BABYLON
OR JERUSALEM

Which Will Rule The World?

Jan Willem van der Hoeven

Publisher's Cataloging-in-Publication
(Provided by Quality Books, Inc.)

Van der Hoeven, Jan Willem.
  Babylon or Jerusalem : which will rule the world? /
Jan Willem van der Hoeven. — 1st rev. ed.
    p. cm.
  Includes bibliographical references.
  LCCN 2009905135
  ISBN-13: 9780942507829
  ISBN-10: 0942507827

  1. End of the world. 2. Church and politics.
3. Zionism. 4. Christian Zionism. 5. Arab-Israeli
conflict. 6. Israel--Relations--Arab countries--
Religious aspects. I. Title.

BT877.H64 2009   236.9
                     QBI09-600117

Personal correspondence should be directed to:
Jan Willem van der Hoeven
International Christian Zionist Center
P.O. Box 49063 • Jerusalem 91490, Israel
Telephone: 972-(0)2-997-8808 • Fax: 972-(0)2-997-1659
Email: iczc@iczc.org.il • Ministry website: www.israelmybeloved.com
Wholesalers and retailers, please direct orders to the publisher, as well
as individuals in the United States who wish to obtain this book:

Deeper Revelation Books
P.O. Box 4260 • Cleveland, TN 37320
Phone: 423-478-2843 • Fax: 423-479-2980
www.deeperrevelationbooks.org

Distribution information posted on the website
Deeper Revelation Books assists Christian authors in publishing and
distributing their books. Final responsibility for design, content, editorial accuracy,
and doctrinal views, either expressed or implied, belongs to the author.

Contents

Acknowledgments

Foreword

Introduction

Part 1 Babylon

Chapter One   The Beginning of Babylon 9

Chapter Two   The Economic Factor 13

Chapter Three   The Political Factor 19

Chapter Four   The New Age Spiritual Factor 29

Chapter Five   Will History Repeat Itself? 45

Chapter Six   What Role Will the Church Play? 55

Part 2 Jerusalem

Chapter Seven   Jerusalem, God's Focal Point for a
                 New World 83

Chapter Eight   The Time of Jacob's Trouble 89

Chapter Nine   Early Christian Zionists 115

Chapter Ten   The Jewish Zionists 123

Chapter Eleven   Why Israel Is Hated 139

Chapter Twelve   The Battle for the Land 157

Chapter Thirteen The Temple Mount 177

References   187

Acknowledgments

I am thankful to *Deeper Revelation Books'* Mike Shreve, and to my co-laborer and friend Stan Goodenough, for their patient assistance in the editing and updating of this book, a book which I believe to be an important tool to help people understand the significance of the battle that is raging in and around Israel. May it be read by many.

Foreword

We all have our reasons to pray for the peace of Jerusalem. As mayor, mine are self-evident. This book explains other reasons and is written by a man who consistently has prayed for the peace of Jerusalem and shown his friendship and dedication to the Zionist enterprise. With enemies like ours, it is good to know we have such friends.

In 1980, when our parliament, the Knesset, enacted a law declaring Jerusalem the united and eternal capital of Israel, most countries, following a decision by the United Nations, packed up their embassies and left town. There is a Hebrew word—*davka*—which is difficult to translate but denotes paradox: Jan Willem van der Hoeven, *davka*, decided to raise his flag here when most other flags were being lowered. An example of *true* friendship.

We do our best to keep Jerusalem and its holy sites open and freely accessible to all. This is not because the world is judging what it often calls our "stewardship" of the city but rather because we do not want to do unto others the terrible things that have been done unto us.

The Golden Rule (ours is of slightly different wording) is something Judaism and Christianity share. We on our part will always be willing to share the beauty of splendor of this ancient/modern city with friends who consistently have shown that, even when things look black, they are right there alongside us anticipating the coming dawn.

Teddy Kollek
(Mayor of Jerusalem, 1965-1993)

Introduction

Two cities figure predominantly in the Bible's discussion of the end times: BABYLON and JERUSALEM.

- One represents man's attempt to make a perfect world on his own; the other, God's intervention and salvation.

- One symbolizes man's drive for prosperity, stability and unity without God; the other, God's impartation of these things through submission to His Lordship.

- One is a city full of greed, materialism and immorality; the other, a city filled with selflessness, peace, and holiness.

- One is the seat of a cruel megalomaniac: a world dictator who talks of peace and prosperity, but will finally be revealed as a false messiah. The other is the seat of the true Prince of peace, whose reign will bring ultimate peace and righteousness to this world.

Part 1

Babylon

Chapter One

The Beginning of Babylon

The beginning of Babylon was Babel. The story of its origin is told in the first book of the Bible,

Now the whole earth had one language, and one speech.
Genesis 11:1

Because people were united and had only one language, they believed they could do anything without the help of God. Men said,

Come, let us build ourselves a city, and a tower whose top is in the heavens; let us make a name for ourselves...
Genesis 11:4

It was for this reason that God came down, confounded their language and thus created different nations. The evil one, who desires to unite mankind under his influence, has always hated this barrier of nationality that God created to prevent man from uniting in rebellion against Him.

By giving them each a different language, God caused them to be scattered as separate nations across the earth. Satan knows that if he is to reign fully over humanity, he must find a way to overcome this barrier of nationality used by God to divide a once united mankind.

We are living in an age when this is happening. This has been the century of world wars. The governments and leaders of this world have been singularly confronted by the necessity to unite in order to survive. The immense problems of this present time—war, the spread of nuclear weapons, increasing environmental pollution, starvation and epidemics, the dissipation of man's resources, overpopulation, financial crises—all cry out for global solutions and appeal for an institution capable of enforcing such solutions—in fact, a world government.

We have already witnessed this trend. At the end of the First World War, in 1917, the League of Nations was established; it was the forerunner of the United Nations. Following World War II, the United Nations was formed to manage mankind's problems. It will take only one more global or serious territorial conflict to compel the creation of a world government.

Tremendous forces, influences and rationalizations have synchronized to increasingly impress upon the minds of most reasoning politicians and economic specialists of our time that the only solution to the enormous and ever-expanding problems of this world is a world federation or world government.

In the following chapters we will see some of these forces and influences at work on:

- the political plane;
- the economic and financial plane;
- the ideological plane; and
- the religious or spiritual plane.

The works referenced in this book indicate just how extensive this movement toward a global government is.

In his excellent book, *En Route To Global Occupation*, Gary Kah reveals how transcontinental economics, global politics, the New Age movement, Freemasonry, the secret teachings of the New World

Order and the coming world crisis all cry out for a global solution, which in all probability will lead to the formation of some kind of world government.

Concluding his book, Kah counsels his readers to write to their legislative representatives as follows:

> As a citizen of the United States of America (or other nation) whose rights are protected by our unique constitution, I do not wish to become a "World Citizen" placed under the authority of a world government and a world constitution. It is not the obligation of this country to come under the rule of the United Nations or any subsequent global government body. To do so would not only be un-American and unconstitutional, but extremely dangerous to the religious and political freedoms of our citizens. I therefore urge you to do whatever possible in your position of power to protect the sovereignty of this nation.(1)

We can, therefore, recognize the vital necessity of being alert to the creeping, all-pervasive danger of downplaying our national sovereignties in favor of a new world order or world government. This is what the evil one has incessantly sought to accomplish since the Tower of Babel. As we shall see, he is using a diversity of ways to achieve his goal!

Chapter Two

The Economic Factor

One of the primary means being used to forge a world institution or government is the economic factor.

The United States of America's bank notes are printed and owned by the Federal Reserve Board. Established on Jekyll Island, off the coast of North Carolina, the Board, since its inception, has consisted of some of the world's most influential bankers. Among its first members were Senator Nelson W. Aldrich, National Monetary Commission; Henry P. Davison of J.P. Morgan and Company; Frank A. Vanderlip, president of the National City Bank; A. Piatt Andrews, Assistant Secretary of the Treasury; and Paul Warburg of Hamburg, Germany, one of the most powerful and influential among them.

One of the first powerful banks with a global outlook was the Morgan Bank. Ron Chernow wrote probably the most definitive and extensive book on this powerful and influential House of Morgan.(2) Global control and outlook already were present in embryo in this powerful banking house and later further developed, with the cooperation of other famous banks, in the creation of the Federal Reserve Board.

William Greider wrote,

As an economic institution, the Federal Reserve inherited
the noblesse-oblige role that the House of Morgan could
no longer perform.(3)

Congressman Louis McFadden said that, when the Federal
Reserve Act was passed,

...the people of these United States did not perceive
that a world banking system was being set up here. A
super-state controlled by international bankers and international industrialists acting together to enslave the
world for their own pleasure. Every effort has been
made by the Federal Reserve to conceal its powers, but
the truth is the Federal Reserve has usurped the Government. It controls everything here and it controls all our
foreign relations.(4)

McFadden's words run strikingly close to those of President
Woodrow Wilson, who said,

There is a power somewhere so organized, so subtle, so
watchful, so interlocked, so complete, so pervasive, that
they better not speak above their breath when they speak
in condemnation of it.(5)

Morgan was a famous banker and major supporter-ally of the New
World Order. His family, says Ralph Epperson in *The Unseen Hand*,

...had a long history as supporters of globalism, stretch-
ing all the way back to Alexander Hamilton, who was
the first U.S. Treasury Secretary and Morgan's distant
relative.(6)

Yet, before the Federal Reserve Board was formed, the Morgan
Bank held a lot of the influence which would later be transferred to
the Board, while much of the bank's special flavor issued from its
global perspective. Chernow writes that,

...as a conduit for capital transfers between America and Europe, the old House of Morgan had naturally looked abroad and was uniquely cosmopolitan at a time when America was still provincial and isolationist. *Now the rest of the country had caught up.* The Morgan bank's foreign connections, once incomparable, might today be matched by those of many foreign ministries, central banks, or even multinational corporations.(7) (Emphasis added.)

The pre-1935 House of Morgan was probably the most influential bank in history. It was also the most secretive with its bankers, power brokers and unofficial governmental representatives at international conferences. Its power was awesome.

Some 78 major corporations, including many of the country's most powerful holding companies, banked at Morgan. Pierpont (the first Director) and his partners in turn held 72 directorships in 112 corporations, spanning the worlds of finance, railroad, transportation, and public utilities.(8)

Furthermore, Wall Street bankers

...incestuously swapped seats on each other's boards. Some banks had so many overlapping directors it was hard to separate them.(9)

No one had been more emboldened by the new financial power than President Woodrow Wilson, who was "eager to underwrite liberal dreams with Wall Street money."(10)

During this period, Tom Lamont (a Morgan partner), acquired his keen interest in foreign affairs. In 1917, he was already traveling with Colonel (Edward) House to Europe to study the European situation.(11)

Lamont became a fervent believer in the League of Nations vision espoused by Wilson and channeled substantial finances to organizations supporting American entry into the League. Epperson writes, concerning Colonel House, that he created Woodrow Wilson [and] he also was involved in making Franklin Roosevelt the President of the United States.(12)

House had written the book *Philip Dru, Administrator* in 1912, in which the hero gave America "Socialism as dreamed of by Karl Marx."(13)

The character of Dru also rewrote the "obsolete...and grotesque Constitution of the United States," says Epperson,(14) adding that during the early months of 1907, J.P. Morgan was in Europe apparently to have the Morgan Bank precipitate a bank panic in America, which eventually would lead to the preeminence of the banks within the Morgan orbit.(15)

Scribner's *Concise Dictionary of Biography* says of Colonel House:

> No other American of his time was on such close terms with so many men of international fame.

As Pat Robertson writes in *The New World Order,*

> Beyond State socialism, House wanted a one-world government, a one-world army, a one-world economy under an Anglo-Saxon financial oligarchy, and a world dictator served by a council of twelve faithful men.(16)

According to Charles Seymour, Colonel House's biographer, the Colonel was "the unseen guardian angel" of the Federal Reserve Act. James Perloff, in *The Shadows of Power,* states that an

> ...objective specified in Philip Dru (the book written by Col. House) was a "league of nations." This, of course, was precisely the name given to the world body created at Woodrow Wilson's suggestion during the 1919 Paris Peace Conference. Just as the 1907 Panic was employed to justify a central bank, so was World War I used to justify world government.(17)

To the Paris conference, Wilson brought his famous "Fourteen Points." The fourteenth carried the payload,

> ...a proposal for a "general association of nations." From this sprang the League of Nations. It was the first step toward the ultimate goal of the international bankers: a world government—supported, no doubt, by a world central bank.(18)

Incidentally, Colonel House was also one of the founding members of the Council of Foreign Relations (CFR); the council's founding president was John W. Davis, J.P. Morgan's personal attorney and self-made millionaire.

William Greider, in *Secrets of the Temple: How the Federal Reserve Runs the Country,* writes,

> One of the damning complaints against the Federal Reserve, from the beginning, in 1913, was that it became the captive of the largest banks in Wall Street and the other financial centers.(19)

So, whether by necessity or willful design, men of finance are steering this world more and more toward a global economic unit. They do not doubt that for the world, in its present predicament, this truly is the best course to take!

Say the researchers,

> If the exercise of power were measured in terms of how swiftly and intimately it altered the behavior of others, then the Federal Reserve was *arguably the most powerful instrument of government,* certainly in the realm of economic behavior.(20) (Emphasis added.)

> If the key to controlling a nation is to run its central bank, one can imagine the potential of a *global* central bank, able to dictate the world's credit and money supply. The roots for such a system were planted when the

International Monetary Fund (IMF) and World Bank were formed at the Bretton Woods Conference of 1944. These UN agencies both were CFR creations.(21)

At the Bretton Woods Conference, Federal Reserve Board governor, Marriner Eccles, already noted,

An international currency is synonymous with international government.(22)

Thus, the influences at work in the world of high finance are considerable, and they combine into one of the extremely powerful factors contributing to the internationalization already seen in the World Bank and International Monetary Fund and will, in the near future, intensify the drive toward some kind of world government.

We have seen how the financial and economic crises are steadily leading men of influence and wealth to an increasingly global approach in their handling of these problems, which will finally result in a worldwide structure or government.

We shall see that many men of political influence and power are coming to the same conclusions in the light of the horrendous political problems confronting this world.

Chapter Three

The Political Factor

*T*here are different organizations in the world working toward a similar goal—some type of global government to which nations will submit, for the common good, their individual sovereignty. The prevailing mindset will be that we are not first and foremost citizens of our individual countries, but citizens of and fellow dwellers in this global village, Earth.

Some of the organizations that, for varying degrees of time, have been working toward attaining this goal are:

- The Council of Foreign Relations (CFR)
- The Institute of International Affairs (IIA)
- The Trilateral Commission
- The Bilderbergers
- The Club of Rome
- The United Nations
- The World Constitution and Parliament Association

These are but a few of the most important, quasi-political structures using their influence and prestige to prepare the world for the eventuality of a world government. They are all, in some way or another, working toward achieving a more globally oriented solution to mankind's problems.

Certainly, the members of these organizations are not all evil individuals with ambitions stemming from heinous or sinister motives, although some may have personal ambitions for greater influence and power. Rather, there is generally an earnest desire to see this world function better, and they honestly believe that in order to realize this, there will have to come into being a global structure that can handle and solve man's seemingly insurmountable problems.

The trouble, however, with this "vision" for the future is this— that in pursuing these things in their own wisdom and strength, powerful individuals have increasingly become pawns in the hand of the evil one who, without their knowledge, has his own grand designs for the future of planet Earth. The Bible forewarns, "...the mystery of lawlessness is already at work..." 2 Thessalonians 2:7

Let's take a closer look at some of these organizations:

The Council on Foreign Relations

In *The Shadows of Power,* James Perloff writes,

Well before the Senate's vote on ratification, news of its resistance to the League of Nations reached Colonel House, members of the Inquiry, and other US internationalists gathered in Paris. It was clear that America would not join the realm of world government unless something was done to shift its climate of opinion. Under House's direction, these men, along with some members of the British delegation to the Conference, held a series of meetings. On May 30, 1919, at a dinner at the Majestic Hotel, it was resolved that an "Institute of International Affairs" would be formed. It would have two branches— one in the United States, one in England.

The American Branch became incorporated in New York as the Council on Foreign Relations on July 29, 1921....

Colonel House, of course, was one of the CFR's founding members...

...the British branch became known as the Royal Institute of International Affairs.(23)

The CFR founders were also uniquely identified by their association with J.P. Morgan and Company. Georgetown professor, Dr. Carroll Quigley, labeled the CFR "a front group for J.P. Morgan and Company, in association with the very small American Round Table group."(24)

As Perloff writes,

The founding president of the CFR was John W. Davis, who was J.P. Morgan's personal attorney and a millionaire in his own right. Founding vice-president was Paul Cravath, whose law firm also represented the Morgan interests. Morgan partner Russell Leffingwell would later become the Council's first chairman.(25)

Although the Morgan interests dominated the CFR in its early days, the center of influence gradually shifted to the Rockefellers, with David Rockefeller holding chairmanship of the Council between 1970–1985.

There is no doubt that,

...while the Council maintains an extraordinarily low profile, it is not a secret society.(26)

Dr. Quigley, himself a member, called the CFR "a front group," while historian, Arthur Schlesinger, Jr., referred to it as a "front organization." It is helpful to understand it in these terms.

In the barely known story of the most powerful family in America, *The Rockefeller File*, Gary Allen writes,

The Insiders cloak their grasp for world political power in many idealistic cliches, and hide their true intentions behind a number of code phrases. The current favorite seems to be "New World Order."

This expression is as old as the diabolical scheme of a secret society of the Eighteenth Century, called the Illuminati, for a *novus ordo seclorum*—in fact, "new world order" is merely a translation of the Illuminati's avowed goal.(27)

No wonder former governor of New Hampshire, Meldrim Thomson, Jr., in his recommendation to Perloff, writes,

If we want to avoid the disaster of one-world government, if we wish to preserve our priceless national sovereignty and live through all time as free men, then it is imperative that the American people read *The Shadows of Power.*(28)

The Trilateral Commission

During 1973, David Rockefeller asked some 200 leading bankers, businessmen, politicians and labor leaders throughout the world to form with him The Trilateral Commission.

Zbigniew Brzezinski, former national security advisor to President Jimmy Carter, became the Commission's first director. Brzezinski, who was already a member of the CFR, wrote in the Council's official journal, *Foreign Affairs,*

The world is not likely to unite (willingly) behind a common ideology or a super-government. The only hope is that it will now respond to a common concern for its own survival. Today the Atlantic framework is too narrow to encompass the multitude of challenges—and opportunities—that confront the international community. It is a recognition of this reality to propose that the active promotion of such trilateral cooperation must now become the central priority of U.S. policy.(29)

In his book, *Between Two Ages,* Brzezinski tried to prove that

...national sovereignty is no longer a viable concept, [and that] Marxism represents a further vital and creative stage in the maturing of man's universal vision.(30)

We shall see again and again, expressed by all these people, the attack is on sovereignty or nationality—the very thing that God created to prevent this horizontal, one mankind unity.

God's barrier of nationality has to be overcome in favor of a new world order in which citizens, even if they will not speak the same language, will be made to realize that they are first and foremost citizens of this global village, Earth.

Professor Richard Gardner, who is a member of the Council on Foreign Relations and the Trilateral Commission, wrote in *Foreign Affairs:*

> Attempts to achieve instant world government must be changed. An end-run around national sovereignty eroding it piece-by-piece will accomplish more than the old-fashioned frontal assault.

In the quotations on the following pages this same idea—down with nationality, up with a new world consciousness—is expressed in various forms: An article in *Foreign Affairs* (December 1922), mouthpiece of the CFR, reads:

> Obviously there is going to be no peace or prosperity for mankind so long as it remains divided into fifty or sixty independent states. Equally obviously there is going to be no steady progress in civilization or self-government among the more backward peoples until some kind of international system is created which will put an end to the diplomatic struggle incident to the attempt of every nation to make itself secure. The real problem today is that of world government.

The Club of Rome

The Club of Rome is an organization claiming to hold the formula for world peace and prosperity, but its solutions habitually promote the world government concept over individual national sovereignty. In its inaugural meeting in the Italian capital in 1968, the

Club, represented by leaders from ten different countries, proposed dividing the world into ten governing units or kingdoms, as follows:

- **Region I**, North America (including Canada)
- **Region II**, West Europe
- **Region III**, Japan
- **Region IV**, Australia (including Israel, South Africa, New Zealand)
- **Region V**, East Europe (including Russia)
- **Region VI**, Latin America
- **Region VII**, Middle East (all the Arab nations)
- **Region VIII**, Tropical Africa (all the black African nations)
- **Region IX**, South Asia (including India, the Philippines, etc.)
- **Region X**, China, etc.

The Club, which includes top influential scientists, educators, economists, humanists, industrialists and important civil servants—a high percentage of whom were drawn from the CFR—intermittently forwards highly confidential reports to the power-elite.

Aurelio Peccei, the Club's founder, stated,

Their world model, based on new developments of the multilevel hierarchical systems' theory, divides the world into ten interdependent and mutually interacting regions of political, economic or environmental coherence.(31)

Here one asks whether this division could be what Daniel the prophet saw represented in his apocalyptic visions, in which the final world power was seen divided into ten kingdoms. (See Daniel 2:41 and 7:7.)

The Bilderbergers

Gary Kah explains in *En Route to Global Occupation* that the overriding purpose of the Bilderbergers, like that of its sister organizations the Council on Foreign Relations and the United Nations, "...is the establishment of a world government." Prince Bernhard of the Netherlands, the group's first chairman, wrote,

Here comes our greatest difficulty. For the governments of the free nations are elected by the people, and if they do something the people don't like they are thrown out. It is difficult to re-educate the people who have been brought up on nationalism to the idea of *relinquishing part of their sovereignty* to a supernational body...This is a tragedy.(32) (Emphasis added.)

Prominent Bilderbergers have included former U.S. Secretary of State Henry Kissinger, former Swedish Prime Minister Olaf Palme, former Prime Minister Barend Willem Biesheuvel of The Netherlands, former U.S. President Gerald Ford, former Chancellor Helmut Schmidt of Germany, Italy's Mariano Rumor, former French President Giscard d'Estaing, former U.S. Ambassador to the United Nations and President Barack Obama's special envoy to Afghanistan and Pakistan, Richard C. Holbrooke, former Secretary of State Condoleezza Rice; former U.S. Special Middle East Coordinator Dennis B. Ross, former Secretary of State George P. Shultz, Sweden's former Prime Minister and Minister of Foreign Affairs, Carl Bildt, and Germany's former Vice Chancellor and Minister of Foreign Affairs, Joschka Fischer. (33, partial source)

Adam Weishaupt, founder of the notorious Illuminati, a secret society created on May 1, 1776, wrote,

With the origin of nations and peoples the world ceased to be a great family.... Nationalism took the place of human love.(34)

Again, we see here the resentment against God's erected barrier of nationality. Epperson reveals Weishaupt's belief in the need for a world government to replace national governments.

The League of Nations was formed after the First World War, and following World War II the United Nations was established. Each time, the catastrophe of a global conflict was needed to force mankind into accepting that only through an international body or government could man ever hope to escape the seemingly endless cycle of wars and disaster.

Will it take a third world war or universal catastrophe for the international community to accept the Club of Rome's blueprint— a world presidium or government of ten presidents (or kingdoms), into which the earth has already been portioned by those who believe they can bring about an end to man's suffering?

Will that be the ten-headed beast that Daniel and John the apostle saw and described—the world government from which an evil world dictator eventually will arise? (See Daniel 7:24–27 and Revelation 13.)

The United Nations

It is perhaps appropriate here to relate some of the history and evolution of the United Nations, which, in many respects, may be the forerunner of a world government to come.

In his book on the international organization, Robert W. Lee writes,

> ...for thirty years we have been asked to believe that an international union under the economic, political, cultural, geographic and linguistic *Tower of Babel* on New York's East River can save us from the scourge of war and protect our personal liberties! It is an incredibly unrealistic and dangerous assumption.(35)

> On United Nations Day in 1975, the World Affairs Council of Philadelphia unveiled the notorious "Declaration of INTERdependence" authored by internationalist historian Henry Steele Commager. The document called for "all nations to strengthen and to sustain the United Nations," and claimed that "To establish a new world order" it "*is essential that mankind free itself from the limitations of national prejudice....*"(36) (Emphasis added.)

Joseph Clark, the former president of the United World Federalists, and former Pennsylvania senator said, "Old fashioned patriotism is surely an obstacle to world government."(37)

That is exactly what God intended when He divided the people into different nationalities to prevent such unity at Babel. But even so, the United Nations is only a preliminary step on the road toward a final world government, as different internationalists have themselves stated over the years,

Although the ultimate need for an organisation stronger than the United Nations must be clear to any thoughtful observer, the question of what type of organisation is realistically possible at the present time is the real issue... In other words, time—a long time—will be needed before world government is politically feasible.... Allen W. Dulles (CFR) and Beatrice Pitney Lamb(38)

John Foster Dulles, Allen's brother and himself a CFR member, who became President Dwight Eisenhower's first secretary of state, wrote,

The United Nations represents not a *final* stage in the development of world order but only a primitive stage. Therefore its primary task is to create the conditions which will make possible a more highly developed organization.(39) (Emphasis added.)

Philip Isley, a founder of the World Constitution and Parliament Association, reportedly said of these "problems which threaten to destroy or severely cripple the future of all people on earth" that they "cannot be solved on a local basis nor by negotiations by sovereign nations, whether inside or outside of the United Nations."

As we have already noted, these "conditions" for which the world is waiting may well arise after a third world war or conflict forces the nations to accept the then inevitable solution—a United Nations upgraded into a world government with ten presidents, each presiding over one of the ten regions into which the erudite and influential men of the Club of Rome have already divided mankind.

Nate Krupp in *The Omega Generation?* concisely sums up the trend toward a one-world government,

Man's tendency to look to big government to solve its problems, ultimately leads to seeing a *one-world government* as *the ultimate answer* to the problems of the world.

What are the major problems that man feels he's facing?

1. How to prevent wars from occurring
2. How to have enough food to feed all of the people of the world

3. How to stop, or at least control, the arms race, particularly nuclear weapons

4. How to provide adequate fuel, especially oil, for the needs of the world

5. How to redistribute the world's wealth of money and materials so that all will have ample

U Thant, who was secretary-general of the United Nations, said a few years ago,

> The concept of taxing the rich according to their capacity to pay, in order to cater to the poor according to their needs, is now well established as a simple canon of social justice in all democratic countries.(40)

In 1942, John Foster Dulles, the United States secretary of state from 1953–59, was chairman of the Federal Council of Churches Commission to study the basis of a "just and durable peace." The report he prepared recommended,

> ...a world government, strong immediate limitation on national sovereignty, international control of all armies and navies, a universal system of money, world-wide freedom of immigration, progressive elimination of all tariff and quota restrictions on world trade and a democratically-controlled world bank."(41)

Robert J. Oppenheimer states, "In the field of atomic energy, there must be set up a world power." Dr. Ralph Barton Perry of Harvard said, "One-world government is in the making. Whether we will it or not, we are moving toward a one-world government."(42)

Three ugly forces seemed to have suddenly arisen like giants on man's horizon: exploding population threatening famine, increased pollution threatening poison, atomic weapons threatening destruction. These three seemed to have joined in an unholy alliance to drive all of humanity into a one-world government. More and more men are turning in this direction as the only chance of survival.(43)

Chapter Four

The New Age Spiritual Factor

*S*o far, we have seen how financial and political circles and institutions are leading men to believe that eventually the only solution to mankind's problems will have to be a new world order or world government. There are, however, other currents equally strong in advocating and forcing this idea upon the masses. Some of these are:

1. Increased awareness of these dangers of pollution to our environment, which has led to cries for a strong solution binding on all nations

2. Expansion of nuclear know-how and weaponry

3. The spread of AIDS and other epidemics which, because of the huge expenses involved, need a global structure to fight them

4. The diminishing of man's resources and in some nations overpopulation

5. Famine and starvation in various nations.

Henry Steele Commager wrote,

The inescapable fact, dramatized by the energy crisis,
the population crisis, the armaments race, and so forth,
is that nationalism as we have known it in the nineteenth
and much of the twentieth century is as much of an anach-
ronism today as was States Rights when Calhoun preached
it and Jefferson Davis fought for it. Just as we know, or
should know, that *none* of our domestic problems can be
solved within the artificial boundaries of the states, so
none of our global problems can be solved within the
largely artificial boundaries of nations—artificial not so
much in the eyes of history as in the eyes of Nature.(45)
(Emphasis added.)

One of the concerns often expressed in financial and political
circles is how to envision a fairer distribution of the world's wealth
and material resources.

Again and again, in a glorified humanism independent of any
need for the Creator, we find man rebelling against the only barrier
that God put into place to prevent mankind from uniting against Him
and His purposes. This humanistic philosophy holds that as long as
we can be one or united, we can reach heaven and "make a name for
ourselves." This is much of the thrust toward world unity today, based
largely on man's endeavors, man's ways and man's wisdom.

Pat Robertson writes in *The New World Order,*

Other programs focus on ecological concerns, on hunger
and the politics of food distribution, or on the theories
associated with the new global economics.

Supporting the research and development of all these
programs are some 150 foundations, funding agencies,
and research councils, ranging from Amnesty International
to the World Future Society. Dozens of films and media
resources are already available, from PBS documentaries
to Time-Life films. The services of an immense range of
scholars, statisticians, and scientists are also combined
with those of medical, legal, economics, publishing, and

theology professionals, to help make the entire globalist community one of the most auspicious and formidable emerging industries in the world today.(46)

The concern for our environment and the need to rein in man's greed and misuse of the earth's resources has brought together people from a variety of backgrounds. Then Senator, subsequently Vice President, Al Gore wrote a thoughtful and passionate book on the subject, entitled "Earth in the Balance: Ecology and the Human Spirit." Six years after his defeat in the 2000 election, Gore (according to www.climatecrisis.net) "re-set the course of his life to focus on a last-ditch, all-out effort to help save the planet from irrevocable change," starring in the film, "An Inconvenient Truth." Although not all environmentalists advocate as a solution the establishment of a global power, some, like Professor Richard Falk of Princeton University, do not hesitate to call for a one-world government to deal with this mammoth problem.

Pat Robertson concludes that there are three predominant concerns which stand out in virtually every discussion on the subject:

1. Anti-war and anti-nuclear activism
2. Ecology and environmental protection
3. Emergence of a global New Age religion.

The New Age Movement

The New Age spirituality, more than any other philosophy today, is preparing the mindset of people to accept the concept of a new world order in which mankind will live as "citizens of this global village—Earth." The obvious goal is to live in as much peace and justice as is possible to achieve under the present, near impossible, circumstances. It is this New Age philosophy, so pervasive in the educational and religious sectors, that is extending itself, like a gigantic octopus, all over the world.

One of the main figures to emerge from the Theosophical Society was Alice Bailey (1880–1949), who wrote in her book *Problems of Humanity,*

> The Kingdom of God will inaugurate a world which will be one in which it will be realized that—politically

speaking—humanity, as a whole, is of far greater importance than any one nation; it will be a *new world order*, built upon different principles to those in the past, and one in which men will carry the spiritual vision into their national governments, into their economic planning and into all measures taken to bring about security and right human relations...What we need above all to see—as a result of spiritual maturity—is the abolition of these two principles which have wrought so much evil in the world and which are summed up in the two words: Sovereignty and Nationalism.(47)

In her book *New Age*, Dr. Basilea Schlink quotes Constance Cumbey,(48)

The New Age Movement traces its modern roots to the Theosophical Society, founded in 1875, in New York, by Russian-born Helena Petrovna Blavatsky. "A basic teaching of this organization was that all world religions had 'common truths' that transcended potential differences." The members "believed in the existence of 'masters' who were either spirit beings or fortunate men more highly 'evolved' than the common herd."(49)

Dr. Schlink also quotes Alice Bailey, who was dedicated to New Age thinking and philosophy,

The Plan communicated *via mediumistic dictations* to Alice Bailey consists of the establishment of a New World Order, a New World Government and a New World Religion. The main political goal of the New Age Movement is global control.(50) (Emphasis added.)

Constance Cumbey, in *The Hidden Dangers of the Rainbow*, states that,

...dissolution and/or *destruction of individual nation states* in the interests of peace and conservation [are openly advocated].(51) (Emphasis added.)

Although world domination is the ultimate goal, there are numerous intermediate goals of a political, social and economic nature, including:

- a universal credit card system
- a world food authority which would control the world's food supply
- a universal tax
- a universal draft [in spite of the Movement's pacifist ideas!]
- the establishment of a world economic system
- the replacement of private ownership of credit, transport and staple production with ownership by a world directorate
- the recognition of biological controls on a worldwide basis of population and disease
- a minimum standard of freedom and welfare throughout the world
- a duty of subordinating personal life to that of a world directorate.(52)

Other facets of the movement are:

- Aryanism, i.e., the domination of the Western races; as with Hitler, this is linked with anti-Semitism
- mass planetary initiation, also called "Luciferic initiation," i.e., an act of consecration to Lucifer
- cleansing action, i.e., the extermination of all those who disagree with the Movement's goals
- abortion and artificial insemination
- forced limitation of family size
- genetic control.(53)

It seems appropriate at this point to trace the mystical origins of much of today's modern New Age philosophy. In his chapter on the New Age movement, Gary Kah writes the following:

The religion of the New Age, simply put, is pantheism—the belief that God is the sum total of all that exists. According to pantheists, *there is no personal God*, instead their concept of God consists of what they refer to as a god-force (or life-force). They teach that this energy, or god-force, flows through all living things—plants, animals and human beings. Since this god-force flows through all of us, they rationalize, we must therefore be gods or, at least, part of God.

Because of this belief, most pantheists will automatically support the concept of a one-world government since global unity is essential to the proper flow of the god-force.(54)

And further,

It was interesting to discover that all of the ancient mystery religions from the Bible era were pantheistic. Pantheism originated in the ancient city of Babylon in Mesopotamia and from there spread rapidly in all directions to cover the face of the earth. Hinduism is one of the off-shoots of the original Babylonian pantheism (via the Aryans of ancient Persia). And Buddhism is an off-shoot of Hinduism. *All of the Eastern religions of today are ultimately traceable to ancient Babylon*, where the post-flood rebellion against God began.(55) (Emphasis added.)

Dr. Schlink continues,

At the core of the planned New World Religion is the initiation, openly termed as "Luciferic" not only by David Spangler but previously by Helena Blavatsky and Alice Bailey in their writings. Various leaders of the Movement have attempted to deify Lucifer. According to Alice Bailey, Lucifer is the "ruler of Humanity." In any event, he is the guiding light of today's New Age Movement.(56)

Around 1920, Alice Bailey, herself, established "Lucifer Press" for the purpose of printing and distributing the literature of the Theosophical Society. Because of the public outcry against the name, the publisher soon was renamed "Lucis Press, Ltd."

As Gary Kah observes,

> Until a couple of years ago, Lucis Trust, the parent organization, was appropriately headquartered at United Nations Plaza in New York. It has over six thousand members and is among the many foundations sponsoring the one-world movement.(57)

Dr. Schlink writes,

> The common denominator for the members of the various New Age groups is a counterfeit religious experience: contact with demons through drugs, meditation, psychotechnologies, and other means; and guidance from demonic entities, the masters of wisdom in the planetary hierarchy, from whom the New Age Plan originates. New Agers believe in UFO's and outerspace beings, from whom they reputedly also receive messages. Within the New Age Movement there are groups claiming that Adolf Hitler was one of their number, because he drew his inspiration from the same sources, shared the same goals and employed the same methods.(58)

> A number of the most powerful New Age organizations, such as Lucis Trust and World Union, are well connected with the one-world political societies and feed directly into the World Constitution and Parliament Association (WCPA), the organization charged with the task of actually bringing us into the New World Order.(59)

Just like the Club of Rome, the WCPA's plan includes a ten region world government.

There is an interlocking of membership and aims between the WCPA and the World Union.

> World Union joined with World Goodwill—a creation of Lucis Trust—in 1961. Lucis (or Lucifer) Trust is an off-shoot of the Theosophical Society, which is plugged into the highest levels of Freemasonry. Past and present members of Lucis Trust include: Robert McNamara (who became President of the World Bank), Donald Regan, Henry Kissinger, David Rockefeller, Paul Volcker (who was President of the Federal Reserve) and George Schultz.(60)

We find these same men in the leadership of the Council on Foreign Relations and the Trilateral Commission.

Because of the seriousness of some of these allegations of the New Age Movement's involvement with ideologies of Luciferianism, satanism, occultism, Freemasonry and virulent anti-Semitism, we need to pursue this further.

Gary Kah sees an unbroken line from the ancient mystery religion of Babylon and Egypt, with its occultism and practices of eastern religion, through different stages right up to the Knights Templar, the Rosicrucians, Freemasonry and the Illuminati.(61) Let's, therefore, follow this unbroken line and ascertain whether it really is true.

Speaking about Babylon, we said that its beginning was Babel. The Bible says that Babel—and later the city of Babylon—was located in the land of Shinar. Genesis 10:10

The Jewish historian, Josephus, wrote,

> Now it was Nimrod who excited [the people] to such an affront and contempt of God... *He also gradually changed the government* into tyranny—seeing no other way of turning men from the fear of God...Now the multitude were very ready to follow the determination of Nimrod...and they built a tower, neither sparing any pains, nor being in any degree negligent about the work; and by

reason of the multitude of hands employed in it, it grew very high... *The place wherein they built the tower is now called Babylon.*(62) (Emphasis added.)

In Alexander Hislop's *The Two Babylons,* we find the following passages:

> If the founder of Babylon's glory was "The mighty Hunter," whose name, even in the days of Moses was a proverb (Gen. 10:9), *"wherefore it is said, 'Even as Nimrod the mighty hunter before the Lord'"*—when we find the "Archer" with his bow and arrow, in the symbol of the supreme Babylonian divinity, and the "Archer" among the signs of the Zodiac that originated in Babylon, I think we may safely conclude that this Man-horse or Horseman Archer primarily referred to him.... The Babylonian divinity was also represented very frequently in Egypt in the very same way as in the land of his nativity (Babylon)—i.e., as a child in his mother's arms. This was the way in which Osiris, "the son, the husband of his mother" was often exhibited...It is admitted that the secret system of Free Masonry was originally founded on the Mystery of the Egyptian Isis, the goddess-mother, or wife of Osiris.(63)

Ralph Woodrow, in *Babylon Mystery Religion* writes,

> Much of the Babylonian worship was carried on through mysterious *symbols*—it was a "Mystery" religion. The golden calf, for example, was a symbol of Tammuz, son of the Sungod. Since Nimrod was believed to be the Sungod or Baal, fire was considered as his earthly representation.(64)

> This system of idolatry spread from Babylon to the nations, for it was from this location that men were scattered over the face of the earth (Gen. 11:9). As they went from Babylon, they took their worship of the Babylonian family

(mother and child) and its various mystery symbols with them... Herodotus, the world traveler and historian of antiquity, for example, witnessed the Mystery religion and its rites in numerous countries and mentions how Babylon was the primeval source from which All systems of idolatry flowed...Bunsen says that the religious system of Egypt was derived from Asia, and "the primitive empire in Babel." In his noted work entitled *Ninevah and Its Remains,* Layard declares that we have the united testimony of sacred and profane history *that idolatry originated in the area of Babylonia.*(65) (Emphasis added.)

We further read in Kah's *En Route to Global Occupation,*

...in the Mediterranean where the gospel was accepted in large numbers, in spite of fierce persecution against those who believed...within a few generations there were so many Christians in this region that the high priests of the Mysteries of Greece, Rome, and Egypt began to loose [sic] their control...until finally the occult priests were forced to go underground in order to keep their secret knowledge and traditions alive.... These occult teachings have been handed down from generation to generation ever since, kept alive in the Western world by the secret societies, which are little more than a continuation of ancient occult priesthoods.... As the priesthoods were forced to take on new forms, Gnosticism became a magnet for these occult adepts. Branches of Gnosticism represented the first significant secret societies of the post-resurrection era, with various degrees or levels of initiation and the inner circle of initiates worshipping Lucifer.... Gnosticism flourished through various offshoots such as the Manicheans of the third century, the Euchites of the fourth century, the Paulicians of the seventh century, and the Bogomils of the ninth century.(66)

Kah further relates that at the base of Gnosticism, and especially the teaching of the Bogomils, there was a switching of the roles of Satan or Lucifer and Christ—giving Lucifer more power and glory than Christ Himself.

> It was perversions such as these, handed down in an unbroken tradition from the earliest Gnostics, that were eventually embraced by the Knights of the Temple (Knights Templar) in the twelfth century.(67)

In *The Temple and the Lodge,* Michael Baigent and Richard Leigh indicate that there was a strong link between what later became known as Freemasonry and the early Templars. According to them, the Knights Templar were first created around 1110. The Knights encouraged the popular image of themselves as being in some way associated with the Grail romances—as "guardians" of that mysterious object or entity known as the Holy Grail.

> Amidst the mystique surrounding the Order of the Temple, a number of echoes and images thus became fused. Joshua's army, the Maccabees, and Grail knights merged with yet other historical and/or legendary antecedents— the peers of Charlemagne, the Arthurian Knights of the Round Table and, especially in the British Isles, the Red Branch of Ulster. Nor was martial prowess the only virtue...conferred on them. The Templars appear in *The Perlesvaus* not just as military men, but also as high mystical initiates. This is indicative, for the Templars were only too eager to reinforce the popular image of themselves as magi, as wizards, or sorcerers, as necromancers, as alchemists, as sages privy to lofty arcane secrets.... In their lifetime, then, the Templars cloaked themselves in legend and myth. In their demise, they spawned new legends, new myths, which were then translated by other people into "historical fact." As we shall see, one such particularly potent translation was to be Freemasonry.(68)

There would definitely appear to have been an historical connection between the Jacobites and Freemasonry. Baigent and Leigh even claim that "the Jacobites were the chief custodians and propagators of Freemasonry." Anyway it seems highly significant that Adam Weishaupt, who on May 1, 1776, founded the secret society of the Illuminati, is celebrated in the history of Masonry as the founder of the Order of Illuminati of Bavaria.(69)

All these influences in some way or other have had an effect on and culminated in the religion and philosophy known as the New Age. It comes straight out of Babylon and, in the end, will evolve back into an end-time Babylon which the Bible describes. All these forces now at work will be expressed in a Babylon of permissiveness, the occult and human endeavor.

The final Babylon seen by John while on Patmos is situated in Rome, the city on the seven hills. Also, Peter describes Rome in his time as being Babylon. I Peter 5:13

As Adam Weishaupt and the Illuminati appear to have had such a profound effect on the subsequent movements toward an "elite-dominated" world government, we shall take a closer look at the man and his shadowy organization.

Adam Weishaupt was a Jesuit priest. During his lifetime Pope Clement XIV "annulled the Jesuit Order," an action which apparently aroused his anger toward Christianity and especially toward the Roman Catholic Church. The annulment was ordered on July 21, 1773, three years before Weishaupt founded the notorious Illuminati.

The pope annulled the Jesuit Order because its adherents meddled in political matters, to the annoyance of certain European governments, which complained to the Vatican. As late as February 28, 1982, Pope Paul I told the Jesuits "to keep clear of politics and honor Roman Catholic tradition."(70)

Weishaupt, a Jesuit priest, certainly must have been concerned by the pope's action, possibly to the point where he wished to organize an institution strong enough to ultimately destroy the Catholic Church itself .(7 1)

Weishaupt, himself, wrote,

With the origin of nations and peoples the world ceased to be a great family…. Nationalism took the place of human love….(72)

It is again significant that Weishaupt attacked the very barrier of nationalism that God put up when man united at Babel in rebellion against Him. Weishaupt realized full well that nationalism stood in the way of his accomplishing his sinister ideal—to create a world government ruled by members of his Illuminati.

The pupils [of the Illuminati] are convinced that the Order *will* rule the world. Every member therefore becomes a ruler.(73)

Epperson writes,

In 1777, Weishaupt was initiated into the Masonic Order, the Lodge Theodore of Good Counsel, in Munich, Germany. His purpose in joining was not to become part of this benevolent order, but to infiltrate it and then to control it altogether…As a result the Bavarian government which had discovered the philosophies and purpose of the Illuminati…abolished the order…. One of the countries to which the Illuminati fled was America, and they formed their first chapter in Virginia in 1786, followed by fourteen others in different cities. They organized the Callo-Italian Society, and with the onset of the American Revolution, disciples in America began to call themselves the Jacobins.(74)

In describing the forces and movements which together are working toward a global occupation or world government, Gary Kah devotes one chapter in his book to the Freemasons, which he calls the "hidden catalyst." Having seen that from the days of the offended and evilly inspired Weishaupt there has been a connection between Illuminati, Jacobins and Freemasonry, it would be judicious to study this matter further.

Alice Bailey, deeply involved in the New Age movement, writes in her book *The Externalization of the Hierarchy* the following highly significant passage:

> The Masonic Movement, when it can be divorced from politics and social ends and from its present paralyzing condition of inertia, will meet the need of those who can, and should wield power. It is the custodian of the law; it is the home of the Mysteries and the seat of initiation. It holds in its symbolism the ritual of Deity [sic], and the way of salvation is pictorially preserved in its work. The methods of Deity are demonstrated in its Temples and under the All-seeing Eye the work can go forward. *It is a far more occult organization than can be realized,* and is intended to be the training school for the coming advanced occultists. In its ceremonials lies hid the wielding of the forces connected with the growth and life of the kingdoms of nature and the unfoldment of the divine aspects of man.(75) (Emphasis added.)

As Kah writes,

> Foster Bailey, the husband of Alice, was also involved with Freemasonry and even wrote a book on the organization entitled *The Spirit of Masonry.*(76)

Madame Blavatsky, Bailey's forerunner, was also a member of the Masonic Lodges. Caro Cardinal y Rodrigues, Archbishop of Santiago, Chile, in his book *The Mystery of Freemasonry Unveiled* writes,

> Madame Blavatsky, the promoter or founder of Theosophy in Europe, was also a member of the Masonic Lodges; her successor, Annie Besant, President of the Theosophical Society in 1911, was Vice President and great Teacher

of the Supreme Council of the International Order of Co-Masonry...and among us, in our city, the brother masons are the ones that contribute mostly to spread the Theosophical Society.(77)

The discrepancy between what Freemasons who are still members say about Freemasonry and the revelations of those who have left the lodges is attributable to the fear of breaking the oath of secrecy they have sworn.

Kah writes,

The history of Freemasonry, I discovered, was also the history of the secret societies and the history of the secret societies is the history of organized occultism—particularly in the Western world.... Albert Pike, in his 861-page occult classic entitled *Morals and Dogma of the Ancient and Accepted Scottish Rite of Freemasonry.* Drawing from the sources available to him as the long-time leader of Freemasonry (1859–1891), Pike was able to trace the chronological growth and spread of the Mysteries over the face of the earth *from ancient Babylon down to the presentday Masonic Order.*(78) (Emphasis added.)

Having pointed out the essential dangers of these movements, let me emphatically state that there are many people in them, whether Freemasonry, the New Age or similar movements, who have little or no knowledge about the dangerous and evil origins and purposes of these movements. They are merely seeking a better and more just world and longing for an improved interrelationship for mankind.

Chapter Five

Will History Repeat Itself?

After all that has been revealed thus far, some might still belittle amassed evidence as overemphasized hogwash or alarmist demagoguery. For their sakes especially, let us see how similarly rooted philosophies and people have led, in the past, to terrible regimes, like that of Hitler's, and could well, in the future, give rise to a similar, if not more evil, dictator.

I quote extensively from the book *The Twisted Cross*, whose author, Joseph Carr, studied the influence of the occult on Adolf Hitler.

> The Thule Society had such a profound effect on Adolf Hitler that it can be claimed that this little band of occultist nuts literally changed world history. They had an influence on history that is far out of proportion to their numbers or importance.

> The occultic ideas pursued by Adolf Hitler were not new, nor did they die with Hitler.... Like the so called "New Agers" of today, Hitler sought an evolutionary leap to a new species of man who is called by New Agers today *homo noeticus.*

Today's New Age Movement, led by disciples of Alice A. Bailey, professes almost exactly the same worldview as did the Nazis.(79)

Among the books that Hitler kept at his bedside and annotated heavily was *The Secret Doctrine* by Madame Helena P. Blavatsky. As Carr notes,

> *The Secret Doctrine* was introduced to Hitler by Dietrich Eckart during the early 1920's, and he was taught its secrets by Professor-General Karl Haushofer.(80)

> Secret occultic societies were numerous in Germany during and right after World War I. Some of them were Rosicrucian in nature, while others were fashioned after the Theosophists. Others, such as the *Hammer Union* and the *Wandervogel* were hyperpatriotic nordic racist cults that idolized the nordic gods of pre-Christian Germany. Only a few seemed to have been deeply rooted in forbidden occultic teaching, and most of those groups used the writings of Madame Blavatsky as their "bible." *Among those groups were the adherents to Aleister Crowley's "Magick," the Vril Society and the Thule Society.*(81) (Emphasis added.)

> It is known, however, that the Luminous Lodge (nee: Vril Society) began in France and was associated with French writer Louis Jacolliot (1837–1890). This French writer on the esoteric drew much of his material from occultic sources such as the Swedenborgians. Also associated with the Vril Society was the 16th-century teachings of mystic Jacob Boehme (a co-founder of modern Rosicrucianism) and Claude de St. Martin, a leader from French Uluminism during the early 19th-century.(82)

The earliest records of the Vril Society contain the name of Professor-General Karl Haushofer (Hitler's friend and teacher), who held membership with the society's Berlin Lodge.

In 1918 Haushofer went to live in Munich, which by that time had become a center attracting all manner of occultist and racist groups. These groups formed secret societies, and it was there that Haushofer eventually became a member of the NSDAP or Nazi Party.

Karl Haushofer is widely recognized as the father of the geopolitical theories put into effect by Hitler.

As with most of the occultic groups of Bavaria in the post World War I era, the primary qualification for admission to the Vril Society was minimum competence in Blavatsky's *The Secret Doctrine.* (Blavatsky was extremely influential in the wording of the philosophy of the New Age movement.)

Karl Haushofer was alleged to be a master of the secret doctrines espoused by Blavatsky, and it was he who initiated prisoner Hitler at Landsberg Prison.

As both Joseph Carr and Wulf Schwarzwäller state, Hitler probably cracked down on all sorts of occultic groups when he was in power to cover up the fact that so much of his own philosophy was influenced by the occult.

Wulf Schwarzwäller writes this amazing passage in his book, *The Unknown Hitler:*

> A frequent visitor to Landsberg was Rudolf Hess' mentor, General Karl Haushofer, a university professor and director of the Munich Institute of Geopolitics.... Haushofer was not only a well-known geopolitician, he was also inclined toward the esoteric. As military attache in Japan he had studied Zen-Buddhism. He had also gone through initiations at the hands of Tibetan lamas. He soon became Hitler's second "esoteric mentor," temporarily replacing Dietrich Eckhart. In Berlin, Haushofer had founded a secret lodge, the Luminous Lodge or the Vril Society. The lodge's main objective was to explore the origins of the Aryan race and to perform exercises in concentration

so as to awaken the forces of "Vril" which roughly corresponded to the Kundalini energy of the Hindus. Haushofer was a student of the Russian magician and esoteric Gregor Ivanovich Gurdyev. Both Gurdyev and Haushofer maintained that they had contacts with secret Tibetan lodges that possessed the secret of the "superman" (in German: Übermensch). They took the fantasied coming race of supermen quite literally.(83)

In order to find out a bit more about the other society and man who so much influenced the thinking and philosophy of Hitler, namely the Thule Society and the person of Dietrich Eckart, I quote extensively from Schwarzwäller's well-documented study:

> Back in 1912, several German occultists with radical anti-Semitic inclinations decided to form a "magic" lodge, which they named the Order of Teutons [and which] was organized along the lines of the Free Masons or the Rosicrucians, having different degrees of initiation, although it was a sworn enemy to the Marxists and Jews.... [One of the members,] Rudolf Glauer, an adventurer of Silesian origin, who held a Turkish passport and practiced Sufi meditation. . .became the grand master of the Bavarian Order Province and he founded the Thule Society.... The Thule Society got its name from a legendary, prehistoric Nordic civilization. It chose as its symbol the rounded swastika with wreath and swords. The Thule Society is listed in the Munich Association Registry under the rather innocuous-sounding name, Study Group for Teutonic Antiquity. Outwardly, the Society initially posed as a literary circle engaged in the study of ancient German history and customs.

> The "inner circle" of the Thule Society was relatively small and was accessible only to the initiated masters of the esoteric. This is where occult and magic rituals were

performed with great seriousness. There were secret recognition signs, symbols, and all of the paraphernalia of a mythical-esoteric brotherhood. There were crosslinks to the English Brotherhood of the Golden Dawn, *to the theosophists of Madame Blavatsky, and to the notorious magician and adventurer Aleister Crowley.*

The German Workers Party was…founded and controlled by the Thule Society. The Thule was the "mother" to the German Socialist Party.…(84) (Emphasis added.)

Schwarzwäller continues,

The first few months of Hitler's political activity with the German Workers Party were marked by heated debates… the Thule Society was not yet supplying very much money and no one seemed to know how to build up a mass party…all of this changed dramatically at the end of 1919 when Hitler met his mentor, a man by the name of Dietrich Eckart…. Their meeting was probably more decisive than any other in Hitler's life. *Eckart moulded Hitler, completely changing his public persona…* In 1923, shortly before his death, Dietrich Eckart wrote to a friend: "Follow Hitler! He will dance, but it will be to my tune. We have given him the means to maintain contact with them (meaning the "masters"). Don't grieve for me. I have influenced history more than any other German".… Eckart not only was a heavy drinker, he also took drugs including peyote, the South American hallucinogen, which Aleister Crowley introduced into Europe's artistic and occultist circles…. Eckart was also a committed occultist and a master of magic. As an "initiate," he belonged to the inner circle of the Thule Society as well as other esoteric orders. He was once a Rosicrucian and Freemason, but he had broken with them because, as a racist, he could not embrace the internationalism of Free Masonry.(85) (Emphasis added.)

Hitler dedicated his handbook, *Mein Kampf,* to Dietrich Eckart, his magic mentor, whom the Nazi leader even called his "John the Baptizer."

I have focused in some detail on the twin societies, the Vril and the Thule, and the two men especially connected with each, Karl Haushofer and Dietrich Eckart. Just as these philosophies and men could produce such an evil system of government and dictatorship, so similar philosophies of the New Age movement could eventually lead to an equally monstrous system if not unmasked in time. The difference is this time it would be on a worldwide scale, with an evil global dictator of the kind foretold in so many prophecies in the Bible.

Hitler and his *"Dritte Reich"* were, in a way, only forerunners of the worldwide kingdom with its evil king—the pseudomessiah who will begin as a man of peace and worldwide reform, just as Hitler did, before turning into the man of iniquity and war as the Bible foresees.

The prospect is indeed frightening, but as the saying goes, unless we learn the lessons of history, we are bound to repeat them to our own pain and even destruction.

So far, we have seen what enormous financial, economic, ecological, political and philosophical pressures and influences are at work, each of them hammering in its own way to forge what must emerge as a global or one world government—a government under which mankind can live in peace and justice on a higher level.

There is little we can do to prevent this happening. The Bible prophesies that this *will* take place in the end. But it certainly is prudent, and important, to be aware of the tremendous dangers involved, especially in the light of history.

Apostle Paul warns us that the mystery of iniquity *was already at work in his time.* Over the centuries, this "mystery of iniquity" has expressed itself in many different philosophies and persons. Each has risen, claiming to be the saving movement for its nation and society—the French Revolution and Enlightenment under the influence of Voltaire and Rousseau, the Communist Revolution under the influence of Marx and Lenin, the National Socialism of Adolf Hitler. Each claimed, regarding his own movement and ideology, that although there was the need in every case for much blood and violence, the ultimate goal would be a better and more humane society.

The bloody history of both the French and communist revolutions and that of the Nazi regime is well known to us. The death and brutality waiting to be manifested under the New Age Movement, which is hidden in its ideology, is much less apparent, even to many New Age adherents. It is precisely because of this that we need to weigh these matters so seriously.

We may think, as every preceding generation has, that *we* are wiser; that *we* shall not make the same mistakes; that *we* have learned the awesome lessons of the debacles of Hitler, Lenin and Stalin, of Nazism and communism. Nevertheless, we are in danger of falling into the same ravines and traps ourselves, as did the generations before.

Those who regard the Bible as an unsophisticated book—only good for children and old people—will be shocked when they witness the coming about of what it describes in rather precise and colorful detail concerning the horrible end awaiting this world under a one-world government.

Most of the quotations so far have been taken from secular sources. However, they all unmistakably point to the same conclusion indicated by the Scriptures, that in the end there will be a ten-headed monster, or world empire, which will trample upon the whole earth as the prophet Daniel and John on the Isle of Patmos foresaw. With this government will arise a Hitler-or Stalin-like ruler who will believe only in himself and who will have no reverence or respect for God or anyone else.

*...and behold, a fourth beast, dreadful and terrifying and extremely strong; and it had large iron teeth. It devoured and crushed, and trampled down the remainder with its feet; and it was different from all the beasts that were before it, and **it had ten horns**. While I was contemplating the horns, behold, another horn, a little one, came up among them, and three of the first horns were pulled out by the roots before it; and behold, this horn possessed eyes like the eyes of a man, and a mouth uttering great boasts.* Daniel 7:7–8 (NAS, Emphasis added.)

Then comes the interpretation to Daniel:

*Thus he said: "The fourth beast will be a fourth kingdom on the earth, which will be different from all the other kingdoms, and it will **devour the whole earth** and tread it down and crush it. As for the ten horns, out of this kingdom **ten kings will arise**; and another will arise after them, and he will be different from the previous ones and will subdue three kings. And he will speak out against the Most High and wear down the saints of the Highest One, and he will intend to make alterations in times and in law; and they will be given into his hand for a time, times, and half a time"* [i.e., 3.5 years]. Daniel 7:23–25 (NAS, Emphasis added.)

In the light of all that has been written in this and previous chapters, such an evolution of affairs seems highly probable. Much of the human race will not believe that we need God in order to arrive at the right state on this planet or that we need to turn to Him from our own wicked and self-centered ways for wisdom and salvation. Many will refuse his Lordship in both their own personal lives and the world in which we live.

In spite of all the failures of the past, the incredible continues to happen: Man, instead of turning away from himself and toward God for help, rather maintains his belief in his own schemes and endeavors. Completely lost to him is God's often-stated plan, which declares He will cause this earth to become a paradise again—a paradise where nations will war no longer. In that day, according to Scripture, everyone will sit in his garden (under his fig tree) in peace and justice. As the waters fill the sea today, so His glory and righteousness will fill the earth in that glorious day, which is yet to come. (See Micah 4:4, Habakkuk 2:14.)

In spite of all man's failures, though, he still prefers to believe in his own wisdom and his own plans. Sometimes, while adamantly refusing to turn to God, he even erroneously chooses to call for the help of spirits and supposed "higher beings" to accomplish his own designs.

Chapter Six

What Role Will the Church Play?

*N*ot only are secular-minded individuals succumbing to this vision of a unified Babel or Babylon, which incidentally is already under construction. Many professing Christians—who should know better—also have fallen for this global agenda and are willing to put their name and their efforts behind it.

As John saw on Patmos, when the ten-horned beast will finally "come up out of the abyss" Revelation 17:8 (NAS), the apostate Church will sit like a harlot upon that beast. The "mind which has wisdom" should note, that this will take place in a city positioned on "seven hills" (or "seven mountains")—quite possibly a reference to Rome. Revelation 17:8 (CJB, NKJV)

> *And one of the seven angels who had the seven bowls came and spoke with me, saying, "Come here, I shall show you the judgment of the great harlot who sits on many waters, with whom the kings of the earth committed acts of immorality " And he carried me away in the Spirit into*

*a wilderness; and I saw a woman sitting on a scarlet beast, full of blasphemous names, **having seven heads and ten horns**... and upon her forehead a name was written, a mystery, "BABYLON THE GREAT, THE MOTHER OF HARLOTS AND OF THE ABOMINATIONS OF THE EARTH."* Revelation 17:1–3,5 (NAS) (Emphasis added.)

The way in which much of the institutionalized Church has been willing, at times, to cooperate with often the most savage systems of government in history—even the Nazis—leads one to believe that what John the apostle saw certainly will be possible in the future: that at the end of time the apostate Church will sit like a harlot on the ten-horned beast, even though the beast will ultimately turn against and hate this whorish religious system. (See Revelation 17:16.)

To verify this, let us go back in history to see that an apostate Church has shown itself capable of the greatest atrocities and of collaboration with utterly evil systems. Unless we as the Church learn from these sad examples, they may well recur in even worse form and dimension in the near future.

No one who is honest about the failures and atrocities committed by the institutionalized Church throughout history can deny the possibility that what happened, often on an unbelievably large scale, could easily occur again—and certainly will, if we do not humble ourselves and learn the awful lessons of the past.

Already, the traditional Church, in certain parts of the world, has given a hand to murderous terrorist organizations. Sometimes its misguided clergy have even become gunrunners for these organizations!

It was only a few years ago that South African Anglican Archbishop Desmond Tutu came to Israel and the Holy Land for what was a highly politicized visit. On Christmas Eve, when he and his host, Bishop Samir Kafity of St. George's Cathedral in Jerusalem, visited Bethlehem's fields of Ephrata, where the angels once sang "Peace on earth—goodwill unto men!" quite a different kind of chant was awaiting the two bishops of the church. About 8,000 Palestinian youths—organized for this occasion—greeted the clergy with the song: "ANCPLO, Israel—no."

As they chanted, neither bishop rebuked them nor attempted to make them stop. Apparently, it was exactly what was meant to be seen and heard in front of all the television cameras of the world. A pro-Palestinian, anti-Israel slogan became the Christmas message and song the bishops broadcast to the world.

Greek Catholic archbishop, Hilaron Capucci, sported similar colors. After a trip to Lebanon—*allowed by the Israeli authorities, so this "Christian shepherd" could tend his flock in that country*—he was found to be carrying ammunition and explosives in his Mercedes. He used the opportunity to contact PLO terrorists in Lebanon and, in his "church-registered" car, to bring explosives into Israel. Capucci was sentenced to 15 years in prison, but was released following strong pressure from the Vatican, after serving just a third of his time.

After he was freed, Capucci went to Rome, where he held a Eucharist at which he boasted that, after all, he had only been following the example of Jesus—the first *fedayeen* or freedom fighter. Despite these outrageous misrepresentations of Christ, Capucci was not defrocked by the Catholic Church.

Anglican minister, Ilya Khury, personally took two terrorist women to the British Consulate and a supermarket in Jerusalem to plant bombs. As a result, innocent people were killed and wounded. Khury immediately fled to Jordan, where he was made a bishop of the Episcopalian church in Amman. He became a friend of Yasser Arafat and was made a member of the PLO executive even though he was a bishop in a Christian denomination.

(For further information on this very sad chapter of Church history, see the booklet by the Roman Catholic priest and abbot, Leo A. Rudloff, OSB, entitled *Archbishop Capucci and Terrorism.*)(86)

The World Council of Churches—through its Near East Council of Churches for the Middle East and National Council of Churches for the United States—is at least ideologically, often firmly, in the camp of the Palestinian Liberation Movement. Their concern nearly always falls on the side of Israel's enemies, hardly ever on Israel's side. Through their frequently misguided and unilateral statements, they present an evil and negative influence.

Maybe we should not be too surprised about these abominable allegiances of certain individuals in the traditional Church to people or organizations which are sometimes violent or murderous. Hasn't this kind of inconceivable behavior been witnessed often during the long history of the professing Church? Consider—

- the institutionalized Church's involvement in the Crusades with their unwarranted massacres of untold numbers of Jews
- its responsibility for the horrible massacres, tortures and expulsions of innocent men, women and children during the terrible days of the Inquisition
- its sheltering of, and even collaboration with, Nazi murderers and its record of allowing clergy to be openly sympathetic toward the Nazis—giving them free rein to do their awful work?

There is too much to recount, but any accurate Church historian, or studious observer of today's trends in the Church, must conclude that unless we learn from history, we are bound to repeat these horrors again. The result will be a false Church on the side of the Beast, instead of a true Church, manifesting true Biblical Christianity— acknowledging Jesus as the Lord of the Church.

As Bernard Lewis writes,

> From the time when the Roman Emperor Constantine embraced the new faith and Christians obtained control of the apparatus of the state, there were few periods during which some Jews were not being persecuted in one or other part of the Christian world. Hostility to the Jews was sometimes restrained, sometimes violent, sometimes epidemic, always endemic.(87)

Has not the historical Church, in aligning itself with some of these very unchristian and murderous organizations and individuals, become directly or indirectly responsible for the Jewish massacres in history? And more than just Jews have been cruelly mistreated.

Pope John Paul II granted an audience to—and openly welcomed—the terrorist Yasser Arafat no less than four times (September 15, 1982; December 19, 1996; June 12, 1998; February 15, 2000). This unbelievable cordial treatment happened despite the Palestine Liberation Organization's responsibility for untold atrocities in Lebanon (and elsewhere) against Maronite Catholic Christians, whose cries went up to Heaven because of what they suffered at the hands of these murderers.

On May 13, 2009, standing in Bethlehem, the "cradle of Christianity," Pope Benedict XVI told Arafat's successor, Mahmoud Abbas, he strongly supported the creation of an independent Palestinian state in the Land of Israel. So the Catholic Church has been seen as aligning herself with the PLO terror chiefs, as it sided too, through Pope Paul VI, with PLO-supporter and gunrunner Archbishop Hilarion Capucci.

Incredibly, Pope Paul VI, after receiving a letter in which Capucci described his ordeal in prison (a self-inflicted ordeal for his own misdeeds) as having been endured "for peace and reconciliation among the peoples of the Middle East," wrote a warm, personal letter to the bishop, conferring on him "a very special apostolic benediction."(88)

This suffering by mainly Catholic Christians at the hands of the PLO in Lebanon at the same time that the above words were written to the terrorist-loving archbishop only gives credence to the prophetic picture of the harlot that John the apostle describes in his Revelation:

> *The woman was arrayed in purple and scarlet, and adorned with gold and precious stones and pearls, having in her hand a golden cup full of abominations and the filthiness of her fornication. And on her forehead a name was written: MYSTERY, BABYLON THE GREAT, THE MOTHER OF HARLOTS AND OF THE ABOMINATIONS OF THE EARTH. And I saw the woman,* **drunk with the blood of the saints and with the blood of the martyrs of Jesus.** *And when I saw her, I marveled with great amazement.* Revelation 17:4–6 (Emphasis added.)

Let us listen to some of the heartrending cries of Christians who suffered death, agony and torture at the hands of the PLO:

Neil C. Livingstone and David Halevy write in their well-researched book on the PLO the following:

> ...for the most part, Arafat and his lieutenants operate as a multinational crime syndicate, relying on extortion, bribery, theft, narcotics trafficking, and murder to fulfill their financial needs.(89)

This has been very much the grim experience of many Lebanese Christians. Jillian Becker relates the following:

> A young Christian girl, Susan S., who had returned home to Beirut from her university studies in the United States soon after the "civil war," is one of the most mutilated survivors of PLO violence. Extreme as her injuries are, her case is not unique. She was at home with her parents when a number of PLO officers broke in. It remains a mystery why they chose that house, that family, on that night. It may have been a random choice, an act of revenge to be perpetrated on any Christians. The PLO men killed Susan's father and her brother, and raped her mother, who suffered a hemorrhage and died. They raped Susan "many times." They cut off her breasts and shot her. Hours later she was found alive, but with all four of her limbs so badly broken and torn with gunshot that they had to be surgically amputated. She now has only the upper part of one arm. Nuns take care of her in a hospital north of Beirut, high in the mountains. She has asked them to let her die but they have consistently replied that they cannot do that. After the expulsion of the PLO from Beirut in 1982, some Christian women conceived the idea of having Susan's picture on a Lebanese stamp, because, they said, her fate symbolizes what has happened to their country— rape and dismemberment by the PLO.(90)

Eliyahu Tal writes in *PLO: Now The Story Can Be Told,*

Nine American religious, ethnic and educational leaders visited the Christian Lebanese village of Aishiye after the PLO was driven out (Bishop Joseph Sullivan of the Roman Catholic Diocese of Brooklyn and Rev. Carl Flemister, executive minister of 187 Baptist churches, were among them).

Group organizer Malcolm Hoenlein told *The Jerusalem Post* on August 30, 1982, "The group was most moved during their two days in Lebanon when they visited the village of Aishiye. The Christian clergymen were appalled to see a statue of Jesus shot to pieces. The graves of the unfortunate Lebanese were completely desecrated and there was clear evidence that the PLO recently played football with some of the skulls they had exhumed."

John Nasser, 49, is the priest of Aishiye.... He trembled when describing the horrible massacre of his flock by the PLO, comparing it with a similar atrocity committed by the Nazis in the French village of Oradoursur Glane during World War II.

"Nearly 1,000 PLO terrorists attacked our village on October 19,1976.

They rounded up all the people—100 families—and locked them up in the church. Over 60 were left outside. We heard successive machinegun fire followed by dead silence.

We were imprisoned for two days. Then the church doors opened, we saw a horrible picture: 65 bodies of men, women and children lying in a pool of blood. Among them were my brother Ibrahim and my cousin Antony.... Lebanon is full of such Oradour-like hair-raising stories that must be told. The world ought to know what this blood-thirsty foul organization called PLO did to my poor beloved country."(91)

From January 9 to January 23, 1976, the Christian Lebanese town of Damour was surrounded by tens of thousands of Palestinians and Syrians—forces of Sa'iqa—and others. The town was first invaded one night after midnight, when Sa'iqa men dashed into the houses and murdered some 50 people. Father Mansour Labaky, who was able to enter one of the houses the next morning, relates the following:

> ...I remember something which still frightens me. An entire family had been killed, the Can'an family, four children all dead, and the mother, the father, and the grandfather. The mother was still hugging one of the children. And she was pregnant. The eyes of the children were gone and their limbs were cut off. No legs and no arms. It was awful.(92)

When the final onslaught came, on January 23, hundreds of Christians were killed. As Mansour Labaky continues,

> The attack took place from the mountain behind. It was an apocalypse. They were coming, thousands and thousands shouting "Allahu akbar! God is great! Let us attack them for the Arabs, let us offer a holocaust to Mohammed." And they were slaughtering everyone in their path—men, women and children.(93)

The Christian school north of Nabatiye was run by seven nuns before the PLO took over. Sister A told what happened when the PLO came:

> "At first they kidnapped Sister C and raped her. Then they beat the rest of us. We hid in the cellars of the monastery for 18 months. Food was brought at night by the local Christians. For several years the bells of one monastery did not ring."(94)

Susie Assalan, 51, a Beirut widow whose 23-year-old daughter joined the Christian Lebanese Forces to fight the PLO, told *The Jerusalem Post* on August 20, 1982,

> "My best friend, a woman doctor, was dragged from her car three years ago while making a night trip to the

hospital. She was brutally beaten and raped and hasn't been able to practice since."

The PLO have practiced terror for terror's own sake. There is no military objective to be achieved by that kind of thing. It got to the point that a trip to the supermarket had to be planned like a sortie into enemy territory.(95)

It is no wonder that, with all these pentup feelings of hatred and revenge, the Christians in Lebanon turned themselves loose on the men, women and children of the hapless Palestinian population in Shatilla and Sabra when the Israeli Defence Forces were close enough to give them the "courage" to do so. However, instead of blaming the perpetrators—the Christian Phalangists—for this atrocity, the whole world accused the Israelis!

Dr. Ghassan Hamoud, a Sunni Muslim and the owner-director of the largest and best equipped of Sidon's eleven hospitals, had this to say:

> The PLO made me hate them, not because they demanded their wounded to be treated free of charge, nor behaved as if my hospital belonged to them; it was when they broke into the operating theater and forced us to stop surgery and treat their wounded instead—and badly beat one of our doctors who refused to obey them—that I realized they were beasts from the jungle.
>
> They call it a revolution. If so, it is the dirtiest and most wicked, the richest and most brutal one in history. Every junior PLO officer used to race through our streets in a brand new Mercedes with machine guns sticking out.
>
> Their conduct inside the hospital was equally intolerable. Every time a PLO patient needed a nurse, he would simply fire his pistol at the ceiling.(96)

After his release in 1979, Archbishop Hilaron Capucci traveled to Tehran to congratulate the Ayatollah Ruholla Khomeini on the Iranian revolution. This was in complete contradiction to the

Vatican's promise that, after his release, Capucci would stay out of Middle East politics.

Regarding this, we recall what John Laffin wrote about the PLO-Khomeini connection:

> The PLO and the Khomeini regime in Iran share an ideological commitment to the use of terror as a political weapon, and have in common a hatred of the West. Long before the overthrow of the Shah, the PLO supported the Iranian underground with money, arms and training. One of Ayatollah Khomeini's first acts in power was publicly to thank the PLO for its part in the Iranian Revolution.(97)

It, therefore, seems strange that despite Archbishop Capucci's good connections with both the PLO and the Khomeini regime, the Vatican could entrust him, in August 1980, with preventing the closure of 14 Catholic schools in Iran which had come under intense Muslim pressure to be closed. After a successful mission, he was again received by Pope John Paul II, who invited him to further mediate on October 6, 1980.

Direct and indirect Church-condoned violence, even against Christian believers, is not simply a recent phenomenon. The institutionalized Church, in fact has a long history of using violence to attain her objectives or of permitting others whom she used or condoned to do the same. Capucci, let us not forget, was never defrocked, but remained a Church cleric granted audiences and utilized by Pope John Paul II.

In their thoroughly researched expose' on the Vatican's Nazi networks, Mark Aarons and John Loftus tell how the Holy See knowingly aided and shielded Ante Pavelic, the *Poglavnik*, or dictator, of independent Croatia and the man responsible for the horrific massacre of a half million Serbs, Jews and Gypsies.

> Many [of his victims] had been dispatched using extremely medieval methods; eyes had been gouged out, limbs severed, intestines and other internal organs ripped from the bodies of the living. Some were slaughtered like beasts,

their throats cut from ear to ear with special knives.... Many more were simply burned alive.(98)

In spite of these atrocities, Pavelic, as a prominent Catholic leader, hoped for the understanding and support of the Church.

Pavelic also knew that the Holy See looked on Croatia as "the frontier of Christianity"; a special relationship between Croatia and the Pope extended back to 700 AD.

Apart from this strong historical connection, Pavelic was also aware that Pius XII and his senior advisers held extremely charitable opinions of his militant Catholicism. During the war, Pavelic had forcibly converted tens of thousands of Serbian Orthodox under penalty of death. In fact, the atrocities were already underway at the very moment Pius XII received the Paglavnik (Pavelic) in private audience in late April 1941.(99)

Special Agent William Gowen and his colleagues in the Rome detachment of the U.S. Army's Counterintelligence Corps wrote in a final report about Ante Pavelic,

Pavelic's contacts are so high and his present position is so compromising to the Vatican, that any extradition of [Pavelic] would deal a staggering blow to the Roman Catholic Church.(100)

On top of this,

"The British had gathered detailed intelligence showing that Father Krunoslav Draganovic, Secretary of the Croatian Institute of San Girolamo, was the main organizer of the Ratlines used by known war criminals to escape the Western dragnet "(101)

In fact, all the personnel running the smuggling network for Draganovic's Ratline, whereby Nazis escaped to North and South America and to Australia, were Croatian Catholic priests.

Aarons and Loftus conclude,

Apparently the Holy See was not above making profit out of its intelligence operations.(102)

State department records for South America confirm that the Ustashi minister for finance and the French undersecretary of the Vichy Government's state made their way to Argentina via the Vatican supported Ratline.

Rumours of others also surfaced. An FBI copy of a surveillance file—forwarded by Argentina's interior ministry's *Central de Intelligencia*—was cited by Paul Manning as follows:

> ...in 1948, Martin Bormann received the bulk of the treasure that had made up the financial reserve of the Deutsche Bank....Like other fugitives, he entered Argentina in 1948, coming from Genoa on a second-class ticket, with forged Vatican documentation.(103)

In the event this all sounds as though only Catholics failed during and after the Holocaust, let us see how other Christians reacted and behaved.

David Wyman's monumental volume, *The Abandonment of the Jews: America and the Holocaust 1941–1945*, states in its preface,

> This book has been difficult to research and to write. One does not wish to believe the facts revealed by the documents on which it is based. America, the land of refuge, offered little succor. American Christians forgot about the Good Samaritan. Even American Jews lacked the unquenchable sense of urgency the crisis demanded. The Nazis were the murderers, but we were the all too passive accomplices.(104)

Wyman proceeds,

> America's Christian churches were almost inert to the face of the Holocaust and nearly silent too. No major denomination spoke out on the issue. Few of the many Christian publications cried out for aid to the Jews. Few even reported the news of extermination, except infrequently and incidentally.... The Federal Council of

Churches compiled a mediocre record, yet it stood in the forefront of the Protestant effort to help. Besides several public calls for rescue, it sponsored the only nationwide attempt at Christian action, the Day of Compassion of May 1943. But even that event, which most local churches ignored, took place only because Jews urged it on the council and Jewish organizations did much of the necessary work.(105)

Still, today neither the World Council of Churches nor the Near East Council of Churches nor the National Council of Churches hardly ever speak up strongly in concern for Israel. The WCC's silence was deafening when, on the eve of the Six Day War, Egyptian President Gamal Abdel Nasser vowed to drive the Jews into the Mediterranean. Further, WCC statements have often been one-sided in blatant bias toward the Arabs and in condemnation of Israel.

I have related all these things as a warning of what might happen again in the future, unless the Church learns from these lessons of the past and thoroughly repents. She, as John saw on Patmos, may indeed again side with the Beast!

Archbishop Capucci, a prelate of the Catholic Church, embraced the viciously murderous Khomeini without one word of criticism against the evil perpetrated by this man. Could that not be seen as prophetically symbolic of the Church, unless she repents, finding herself supportive of that beastly monster, the antichrist?

With the unbelievable spirit of compromise and openness to deception at work in those who are today regarded as "Christian" (in both the political and religious arenas), one can well foresee the Church finally falling for the ultimate deception and the pseudomessiah.

Even President Jimmy Carter, who publicly claimed to be a born-again Christian, called Khomeini "a holy man," and his representative in the United Nations, Andrew Young, said of the Ayatollah that he was "a twentieth century saint."

As Amir Taheri writes in *Holy Terror,*

Even before the Embassy drama, Tehran knew that some members of the Carter team were fascinated by Khomeini and his revolution.(106)

Richard Nixon also, in his book, *Seize the Moment,* has a passage on Islam that shows a great deal of ignorance and deception. He writes,

Few Americans are aware of the rich heritage of the Islamic world. They remember only that the sword of Muhammad and his followers advanced the Muslim faith into Asia, Africa, and even Europe and look condescendingly on the religious wars of the region. They overlook the fact that Islam has no doctrine of terrorism and that only three centuries have passed since Christians engaged in religious wars in Europe.(107)

Ignorance of the psychology of the members of Holy Terror has not been a prerogative of the United States, however. In 1984 the West Germans sent their Foreign Minister, Hans Dietrich Genscher, to the Islamic republic [of Iran] to lecture the mullahs on human rights. All he received in exchange was a diplomatic slap in the face, while his visit was presented by the official media as a sign that "Satanic forces" were bowing to the power of Islam.(108)

The French did no better:

Another Party of Allah militant to visit Paris with pomp and ceremony was Ali-Reza Moayeri, one of the leaders of the "students" who seized the US Embassy in Tehran in 1979. In April 1986 Moayeri was received by all the top French leaders, including the Prime Minister and the President.(109)

Contrasted with this weak approach and the deceived understanding of the West, the dedication of millions of Muslim fundamentalists seems frightening; not only do they believe in the rightness of their cause, but they state with dogmatic conviction that it is the will of Allah.

Hear the words of Muhammad Taqi Partovi Sabzevari in his *Ayandeh Nehzat Islami (The Future of the Islamic Movement)*, Qom 1986:

> A people that is not prepared to kill and to die in order to create a just society cannot expect any support from Allah. The Almighty has promised us that the day will come when the whole of mankind will live united under the banner of Islam, when the sign of the Crescent, the symbol of Muhammad, will be supreme everywhere.... But that day must be hastened through our Jihad, through our readiness to offer our lives and to shed the unclean blood of those who do not see the light brought from the heavens by Muhammad in his mi'raj...It is Allah who puts the gun in our hand. But we cannot expect Him to pull the trigger as well simply because we are fainthearted.(110)

Khomeini's own formula, "To kill and to die in the service of Allah *is the highest duty of every true Muslim,*" accords perfectly with this.

We now have seen how, in essence, it is possible for a Church that is deceived and decadent to fall for a beastly system or dictator. As indeed in John's vision on Patmos, the beast hated the harlot in return and made her desolate and naked and ate her flesh and burned her up with fire, (See Revelation 17:16.) so too the Nazis and extremist Muslims, although courted by the West and even by many in the Church, have not returned the favor but remain implacable enemies of Christianity.

Those of us who live in the Middle East know the chant of thousands of Muslims as they sing during each war against the Jews, "We shall first fight the Saturday people and then the Sunday people," and they mean it, too! Regardless of this, many in the Church throw themselves into the hands of this unmitigating monster, hoping in vain to "ride it," as John saw the mother of harlots ride the scarlet beast. (See Revelation 17:3.)

Thus, we only need to look to the Church's history to see what might well become reality again tomorrow, unless in deep humility and repentance we learn from the past.

Whether it is in the sad pages of Church history during the terrible days of the inhuman inquisition when thousands upon thousands—sometimes with direct papal approval—were butchered, tortured, burned at the stake, expelled or forcibly converted, all in the name of the Church, or nearer to our time, at the evil collaboration by Church officials with the beast of Nazism or Islam, there is enough evidence for anyone to perceive that such things can happen again. Because the Bible foretells such a scenario, with a totally apostate Church in the end making common cause with the ten-headed Babylonian beast, there is doubly the need for watchfulness.

We now want to sound out just how such a state of affairs may actually come about in the near future.

In his booklet *Ecumenism: Where Is It Leading Us?*, Michael de Semlyen writes,

> In July 1988 the Lambeth Conference of Anglican Bishops Worldwide met at Canterbury and overwhelmingly endorsed the Agreed Statements of the Anglican Roman Catholic International Commission (ARCIC). These statements represent a compromise on the major doctrinal differences between Protestants and Roman Catholics.... Clearly the Roman Church expects unity very much on her own terms. In his new book, "Towards a Civilisation of Love," reviewed in the Christian press in January 1989, Cardinal Hume tells us:
>
> "The Council document on ecumenism is at pains to state: '*The Catholic Church possesses the wealth of the whole of God's revealed truth and all the means of*

grace. It is unable to concede a similar status to others.'"
(Emphasis added.)

When Catholics pray for the restoration of full communion with other Christians, they are praying for that unity which the Church believes Christ willed and which is found in all its essential characteristics in the Catholic Church.

The aim of the ecumenical movement is to bring all churches, denominations, and ultimately all religions together.... In Roman Catholic terminology an Ecumenical Council is an exclusively Roman Catholic affair.(111)

Leading proponents of unity, such as a former Archbishop of Canterbury, Michael Ramsey, described "the whole Ecumenical enterprise as the Holy Spirit working in us, uniting us in love and building us up in the truth." Difficulties over articles of belief were to be put to one side: "We must avoid binding the spirit by our stupidity and narrowness and lack of faith."

Even leading evangelical, John Stott, told the 1977 National Evangelical Anglican Congress (NEAC) at Nottingham that,

...the visible unity of all professing Christians should be our goal...and evangelicals should join others in the Church of England *in working towards full communion with the Roman Catholic Church.*(112) (Emphasis added.)

The charismatic, much loved David Watson, an Anglican minister, said of the Reformation that it was "one of the greatest tragedies that ever happened to the Church."

As de Semlyen states today,

The combination of mass evangelism and the excitement of the Charismatic Renewal had become caught up with and harnessed by the Ecumenical Movement.(113)

With these powerful factors and influences at play, we can hardly doubt the future outcome is a united World Church centralized in Rome. It is, therefore, extremely important to observe which direction Rome will be taking in the coming years. To which forces and influences will she give heed and by which allow herself to be influenced? Will it be the heavenly influence of the Holy Spirit and God's Word or the humanistic influences of the world and the teachings of New Age religion and philosophy, which are already rampant in the Church? This is the question every devout Christian—Catholic, Protestant or Orthodox—should seriously ask.

During one of the most recent conferences in the World Council of Churches in Canberra, Australia, where the theme was "Come Holy Spirit—Renew the Whole Creation," Pope John Paul II said in a message to the assembly that the ecumenical task is urgent because the witness of the Church "is less convincing to the degree that the world continues to be confronted by our divisions." The assembly asked the Vatican-WCC Joint Working Group to concentrate on remaining obstacles to a fuller relationship between the two bodies. It also called for greater attention to relationships with churches outside the World Council of Churches' membership.

The publishers of the extensively researched book by Malachi Martin, *The Keys of This Blood,* write,

Only Malachi Martin, consummate Vatican insider and intelligence expert, could reveal the untold story behind the Vatican's role in today's winner-take-all race against time to establish, maintain, and control the first one-world government.(114)

In his book, Martin describes the tremendously divergent influences at work today within the Catholic Church—influences that either want to undo the Catholic Church of much of its Christian ethics, faith and theology or want to maintain the traditional religious status quo as much as possible.

All who have eyes to see will perceive the tremendous struggle taking place right now in the heart of the Catholic Church. Will it be a church more open to the wisdom and influence of all that rules the world, or will it renew itself in a new commitment to its heavenly calling—to be in the world but not of the world and thus be a gateway to the salvation and reality of God's Kingdom?

The outcome of this struggle is extremely crucial, for if the battle is not won on the side of God, His Kingdom and His Son, then the picture John the apostle had on Patmos will become reality— a church that is not a bride, but an apostate worldly harlot.

To see, therefore, where the church of Rome is headed under today's leadership, it would be good to study John Paul II more closely. Martin certainly does this in his voluminous book on the late pope, arriving at, among others, the same conclusion reached by de Semlyen about the tremendous influence the person of Mary has on this pope and his beliefs.

I first quote from Michael de Semlyen before returning to Martin.

> John Paul II has, as his personal motto, *"totus turn"* (totally yours); but it applies to Mary, not Jesus. Indeed at his enthronement he proclaimed: "...all that I have is thine, my Queen and my Mother." After the attempt on his life in 1981, *Time* magazine reported...that on his way to hospital, he softly murmured, "Madonna, Madonna" in Polish (Tune, May 25, 1981). One year after the assassination attempt, he went to the Marian shrine of Fatima in Portugal to thank Mary for saving his life.
>
> In April 1987 the Pope launched the "Marian Year" to a global TV audience estimated, perhaps generously, at 1.5 billion. Two months later, at a Mass for several hundred thousand people at Lodz in Poland, he prayed to the Virgin Mary *for religious freedom in the world.* In May 1988 in the cathedral at Lima, he consecrated Peru to "Our Lady of Evangelization," anticipating the "decade of evangelism." In Rome, in August 1988, in a ceremony to mark the end of the Marian Year, the Pope proclaimed:

"This is the opportunity to start a Marian walk towards the year 2000. We must walk together with Mary" *(Famiglia Christiana Magazine,* Piedmont, Italy).

The "Our Lady of Walsingham" shrine, at Walsingham in Norfolk, parent to 180 other such shrines in Church of England churches, was host in September 1988 to the BBC programme "Songs of Praise" watched by up to 8 million viewers. 1988 has seen a special pilgrimage to Walsingham organized for some sixty Bishops from the Lambeth Conference as well as the third consecutive pilgrimage from Parliament. Encouraged by the example of (former) Archbishop of Canterbury, Robert Runcie, senior bishops turn out to lead the pilgrimage year after year. Archbishop Runcie, who is President of the Ecumenical Society of the Blessed Virgin Mary, and who according to *Time* magazine, "is probably willing to risk more for the sake of unity than any of his predecessors, is an enthusiast for Walsingham *and its role* in leading the Anglican Church into Catholicism of the Roman kind" *(Time,* June 7,1982).... Many critics of Ecumenism predict that "Church unity under the supremacy of Rome will rapidly lead to a fresh outbreak of bigotry and persecution."(115) (Emphasis added.)

Lest we too quickly judge Pope John Paul for his obvious preoccupation with Mary, rather than with the Lord of the Church, let us consider the tremendous pressures he faced as he tried to steer his church in this present, willful world.

"The claim to build a world without God," the Pope stated bluntly in Czechoslovakia during a visit in April 1990, "has been shown to be an illusion.... Such a hope has already revealed itself as a tragic Utopia...for man is unable to be happy if the transcendent relationship with God is excluded."(116)

What Pope John Paul II was coming up against here were the other movements that want to bring about a new world order without God.

Martin explains how the two Polish cardinals, Stefan Wyszynski of Warsaw and Karol Wojtyla of Krakow, had worked side by side for nearly 30 years in Poland:

> All during these years, the two Churchmen—the Cardinal and the future Pope—already thought and worked in terms of what Wyszynski called the "three *Internationales.*" That was the classical term he used to talk about geopolitical contenders for true world power.

> There exists on this earth, Wyszynski used to say, only three *Internationales.*

> 1. The "Golden *Internationale*" was his shorthand term for the financial power of the world—the transnationalist and internationalist globalist leaders of the West.

> 2. The "Red *Internationale*" was, of course, the Leninist-Marxist Party-State of the Soviet Union, with which he and Wojtyla and their compatriots had such a long and painfully intimate experience.

> 3. The third geopolitical contender—the Roman Catholic Church; the "Black *Internationale*"—was destined in Wyszynski's view to be the ultimate victor in any contention with those rivals.(117)

Martin writes,

On the face of it, the champions of Western capitalism—the Transnationalists and Internationalists of America and Europe—appear to be far and away the most effective and powerful architects of a new world order, for the simple reason that their power base rests on the indispensable pillars of money and technology.(118)

The problem Pope John Paul II, therefore, faced is how the church could make a credible offer for world leadership that would be acceptable, not only to an increasingly secularized, agnostic world, but also to an often compromised Church.

As the German philosopher Martin Heidegger said, "I know that only God can save us."

But the Vatican's dilemma is how to translate this into a recognizable and acceptable solution. How can he proceed without falling into the trap of allowing his church to become so expansive that it will succumb to the exceedingly amoral and rebellious forces already massively infiltrating today's Church?

As Martin writes,

Such in particular are the thousands of New Agers *in our midst*. And such, too, are the so-called Mega-Religionists—those who are persuaded, and who work to persuade us all, that all religions of the world are fusing into one globe-spanning mega-religion of mankind.(119) (Emphasis added.)

The decade of the twenties saw the appearance of more and more mega-religious groups:

- The League of Neighbors (LN), 1920, United States
- The International Fellowship (IF), 1922, India
- International Brotherhood (IB), 1923, Paris
- World Fellowship of Faith (WFF), 1924, United States
- World Alliance (WA), 1924, Oxford, England
- Peace and Brotherhood (PB), 1926, Louvain, Belgium
- The Threefold Movement (TTM), 1926, New York
- World Peace (WP)
- World Conference for International Peace Through Religion (WCIPR)
- Order of Great Companions (OGC)

The last three were established during 1928. Between the mid thirties and the start of the seventies, many more emerged. Some of the more consequential ones were:

- World Congress of Faith (WCF), 1936, London
- The Self-Realization Fellowship (SRF), 1937, Los Angeles
- World Spiritual Council (WSC), 1946, United States
- International Committee for Unity and Universality of Cultures (ICUUC), 1955, Rome
- World Fellowship of Religions (WFR), 1957, New Delhi
- Temple of Understanding (TU), 1959, United States
- Organization of United Religions (OUR), 1967, Paris
- Spiritual Unity of Nations (SUN), 1970, England
- World Conference of Religion for Peace (WCRP), 1970, Kyoto, Japan.

Martin continues,

What John Paul does find disturbing is the degree to which the higher-ranking clergy—cardinals and bishops— throughout his Church organization set an example of Mega-Religionist cooperation for priests and laity alike by joining celebrations *that are intentionally neither Roman Catholic nor Christian.*(120) (Emphasis added.)

His uneasiness is not without reason, as one indeed realizes when reading what the Marxist millionaire publisher and mega-religionist, Victor Gollancz, wrote in 1948:

The ultimate aim should be that Judaism, Christianity and all other religions should vanish and give place to one great ethical world religion, the brotherhood of man.(121)

One wonders what, if anything, will remain of the purity of the bride of Christ—His Body—with these enormous forces and influences at work, both from without and within the Church, and, added to this, the increased moral laxitude and permissiveness condoned in many of those churches currently queuing up to be united—perhaps under the leadership of Rome—in a one-world church.

Yes, she may well include devout priests, nuns, and even Spirit-filled and Bible-honoring Christians. But will she also embrace those who have neither repented from their carnal ways nor come to a true and living faith?

Pope John Paul's battle was horrendous, one would say nearly impossible. As he said on a visit in April 1990 to his Czechoslovakian hosts,

> Almighty God can make the impossible possible, can change all human hearts, through the queenship of Jesus' mother Mary.(122)

Yes, once again let it be emphasized—the vision of John the apostle on Patmos will come true:

> "...I will show you the judgment of the great harlot who sits on many waters, with whom the kings of the earth committed fornication, and the inhabitants of the earth were made drunk with the wine of her fornication." So he carried me away in the Spirit into the wilderness. And I saw a woman sitting on a scarlet beast which was full of names of blasphemy, having seven heads and ten horns. The woman was arrayed in purple and scarlet, and adorned with gold and precious stones and pearls, having in her hand a golden cup full of abominations and the filthiness of her fornication. And on her forehead a name was written: MYSTERY, BABYLON THE GREAT, THE MOTHER OF HARLOTS AND OF THE ABOMINATIONS OF THE EARTH. And I saw the woman, drunk with the blood of the saints and with the blood of the martyrs of Jesus. And when I saw her, I marveled with great amazement. Revelation 17:1–6

As Michael de Semlyen writes,

Apostate Christendom is unifying world religion, which under the surface is as bloodthirsty as it ever was. Once religions of the world combine with the New Age to form one great ecumenical and multifaith monopoly, God's "little flock" will yet again be as lambs to the slaughter.(123) (Emphasis added.)

What I have attempted to show from various sources and by the use of numerous references is just how widespread across a broad spectrum is the drive toward a coming world government. I have shown that the spirit of the world has already entered the professing Church to such an extent—through actors inside both the Vatican and the World Council of Churches—that in some instances there is barely a significant difference between the so-called spirit of unity expressed in the world and the spirit of unity today expressing itself within the institutionalized Church. I am sure that there are still many faithful men and women, both inside and outside of the institutionalized churches—who make up the true, possessing Church. These true believers would want nothing more than to see this world become a better, kinder and more Christlike through the efforts of man, both politically and religiously? The cardinal question, however, is whether the world will truly become better, kinder and more Christlike through the efforts of man, both politically and religiously? Or will we witness, as the Bible foretells, the drives for political and religious unity joining together in the city on seven hills—in an unholy union with the ten-headed world government, with terrible consequences?

One realizes how quickly this all could come about and how the majority of men will nonetheless refuse to believe what a terrible end is in store, until it is too late. But there is another way—a way that is entirely different, and which leads to a city which is entirely different, a city called, Jerusalem.

Part 2

Jerusalem

Chapter Seven

Jerusalem, God's Focal Point for a New World

> *If I forget you, O Jerusalem, let my right hand forget its skill! If I do not remember you, let my tongue cling to the roof of my mouth—if I do not exalt Jerusalem above my chief joy.* Psalms 137:5–6

> *For Zion's sake I will not hold My peace, and for Jerusalem's sake I will not rest, until her righteousness goes forth as brightness, and her salvation as a lamp that burns.* Isaiah 62:1

Just as Babylon is the focal point for a one world government with all the terrible consequences that will result, so Jerusalem is the scriptural focal point for the establishment of God's government on earth—a time when nations will beat their spears into pruning hooks and learn war no more. (See Micah 4:3.) As Babylon will be man's focal point for a new world order, so Jerusalem will be God's focal point for a new and perfect world, in divine order. When this transpires, as the prophets foresaw, *"...everyone shall sit under his vine and under his fig tree, and no one shall make them afraid..."* Micah 4:4 *"The wolf also shall dwell with the lamb...and the lion shall eat straw like the ox.... They shall not hurt nor destroy... for the earth shall be full of the knowledge of the Lord as the waters cover the sea."* Isaiah 11:6,7,9

The Bible focuses on Jerusalem as the city and focal point for world redemption by the intervention of the Lord Himself. For without Him, as Heidegger acknowledged, it is impossible for man to find his way back to the paradise we lost, a paradise of peace and justice.

It is written on the "Isaiah Wall" in front of the UN building in New York, *"They shall beat their swords into plowshares, and their spears into pruninghooks; nation shall not lift up sword against nation, neither shall they learn war any more."* Isaiah 2:4 But that monument is in the wrong place. The Bible does not draw our attention to the vain deliberations of men in New York's UN headquarters as a hope for the fulfillment of this prophetic vision. Isaiah did not see the nations coming up to deliberate in New York as a prelude to world peace and justice. It says, *"The word that Isaiah the son of Amoz saw **concerning Judah and Jerusalem**."* Isaiah 2:1 (Emphasis added.)

It was not in New York that Isaiah saw his vision of a new world and peaceful relationships between nations becoming a reality. Nonetheless, men, in willful ignorance of God's plan, attempt to fulfill the vision there—in vain.

No, the city chosen for this awesome purpose was, is, and always will be—Jerusalem.

No wonder the Bible exhorts us to pray for the peace of Jerusalem. For it is only in this confession of our utter dependency upon the Lord to save us that we will see ourselves and this world saved.

In this respect, it is quite revealing that the least used room in the United Nations building is the prayer or meditation room. In New York, the emphasis is placed on man's endeavors.

There are, therefore, two ways open to mankind—Babylon or Jerusalem. One symbolizes man's trust in his own efforts— that as long as we unite, we can build a new and better world: it is Babylon. The other symbolizes man's dependence upon and trust in God: it is Jerusalem.

After the First World War, man said, "we must unite"—and the League of Nations was born. After the Second World War, man said, "we must unite stronger"—and the United Nations came into being. It may well take the shock of one more global conflict to pre-pare man to upgrade the present United Nations into a ten-headed world government—man's ultimate answer to his insurmountable problems: "Let us unite." This will, as we have already seen, lead to total disaster. In their willful ignorance and rebellion against God, however, people will discover this too late. "We don't need Him or His commandments. We can do without Him!"

And yet, for those who have eyes to see, there is a God at work in this seemingly hopeless world, a God at work to make this earth a paradise of goodness and mercy again. God-loving people have prayed for centuries all over the world that this transformation would take place. These are people from every race, color and nation who—in their personal lives—have not been ashamed to acknowledge that they could have never been saved from their difficulties without calling on the Name of the Lord. With millions of others, these believers have prayed *"Your Kingdom come, Your will be done, on earth as it is in heaven."* Matthew 6:10

One day these people will see a completely restored earth— a new earth and a new heaven in which righteousness will dwell.

But that new world will have only one capital, and that is pres-ently the most despised capital of all—the city of Jerusalem, capital of the reborn Jewish state, Israel.

God always said He would do it; after a long period of disper-sion He would gather His people again from the four corners of the earth, from all the countries where He had scattered them, and bring them once more to His own—to their own—promised land.

God sings and exults through the whole Bible that *He who scattered Israel will surely gather him as a shepherd gathers His flock!* He is so jubilant about it that He says through the prophet that the story of His regathering of His people must be published and proclaimed among the nations, even the islands afar off. (See Jeremiah 31:10.)

Isaiah prophesied,

> *How beautiful upon the mountains are the feet of him who brings good news, who proclaims peace, who brings glad tidings of good things, who proclaims salvation, who says to Zion, "Your God reigns!" Your watchmen shall lift up their voices, with their voices they shall sing together; for they shall see eye to eye when the Lord brings back Zion. Break forth into joy, sing together, you waste places of Jerusalem! For the Lord has comforted His people, He has redeemed Jerusalem. The Lord has made bare His holy arm in* **the eyes of all the nations;** *and all the ends of the earth shall see the salvation of our God.* Isaiah 52:7–10 (Emphasis added.)

This is such an amazing and joyful passage concerning the restoration of Israel. Why is God so jubilant about something most Christians consider of minor interest? Why is this so important to the Most High when many Christians deem it unimportant to their main beliefs of how God is going to redeem this world from final catastrophe? Is it because God saw what Paul would later declare in the glorious 11th chapter of his epistle to Rome—(of all places?) Concerning Israel, His apostle declared, *"if their rejection be the reconciliation of the world [the Gentiles], what will their acceptance be but life from the dead?"* Romans 11:15 (NAS)

Is it because God knew that when His people would come back home for the third time in history—the present return—something so wonderful would result that He has called upon the heavens to rejoice over it and upon those who believe His message to comfort His people Israel? (See Isaiah 40:1-2.)

Sing, O heavens! Be joyful, O earth! And break out in singing, O mountains! For the Lord has comforted His people, and will have mercy on His afflicted. Isaiah 49:13

Even Paul, when he had written his unsurpassed 11th chapter of Romans concerning the final restoration of Israel, ended in a doxology of praise:

Oh, the depth of the riches both of the wisdom and knowledge of God! How unsearchable are His judgments and His ways past finding out! Romans 11:33

Why all this rejoicing by God and by those who have seen the truth concerning God's returning grace and favor to His people, Israel? No wonder God tells the heavens to sing and the earth to be joyful and Paul ends in a doxology of praise when announcing the coming restoration of Israel! It is an event of such dimension and consequence that everyone who has eyes to see and ears to hear will, in response to God's call, rejoice. Yet God has called us to much more than just rejoicing:

- The Lord who comforts His people asks us to comfort His people. (See Isaiah 40:1-2.)
- The Lord who shows mercy to His people asks us to show them mercy. (See Romans 11:30-31.)
- The Lord who will establish Jerusalem as a praise in the earth asks us to pray toward this end. (See Psalms 122:6.)

Unless we understand the full extent of what will result from this restoration of Israel, we will not really rejoice, or work, or pray from our very hearts to see it come to pass. Only when we realize that the redemption of this planet Earth depends on it—that "life from the dead" will result from it, that nations and animals will fight no more following it—will we truly be able, in the fullest sense of the word, to rejoice.

If we fail to understand that the rule of the sovereign Lord will replace the endless cycle of misery and war, we will not be able to rejoice with the God who announces, again and again throughout the Scriptures, the coming of this "day" to His ancient people Israel.

So great is this event that when it takes place,

> ...*the light of the moon will be as the light of the sun, and the light of the sun will be* **sevenfold**, *as the light of seven days, in the day that the Lord binds up the bruise of His people and heals the stroke of their wound.* Isaiah 30:26 (Emphasis added.)

This again is an amazing passage which shows that even the sun and the moon will react in jubilation to the approaching time of comfort for the Jewish people. How wonderful a day that promises to be, if it is announced with such love and heavenly excitement by the God of Israel, who says,

> *With a little wrath I hid My face from you for a moment; but with everlasting kindness I will have mercy on you—* Isaiah 54:8

Chapter Eight

The Time of Jacob's Trouble

"For a mere moment I have forsaken you...." Isaiah 54:7

The pain and cry of this *moment* has been imprinted in a myriad of ways on the pages of Jewish history: from the days when Titus destroyed the city of Jerusalem, to the massacre of Jews following Bar Kochba's rebellion against Rome—through the era of the Crusaders and the subsequent dark and horrifying Middle Ages with its blood libels, massacres and Spanish Inquisition—to the horrifying years of the Holocaust.

It has been a cry drenched in tears, blood and agony. It is a cry still heard from many whose wounds yet have not been healed. Even God acknowledges the appalling severity of this wounding of His people when He says,

> *"Your wound is incurable, and your injury is serious. There is no one to plead your cause; no healing for your sore, no recovery for you. All your lovers have forgotten you, they do not seek you; for I have wounded you with the wound*

of an enemy, with the punishment of a cruel one, because your iniquity is great and your sins are numerous...your pain is incurable." Jeremiah 30:12–15 (NAS)

Yet God ends this passage with these words:

"Therefore all who devour you shall be devoured; and all your adversaries, every one of them, shall go into captivity; and those who plunder you shall be for plunder, and all who prey upon you I will give for prey. For I will restore you to health and I will heal you of your wounds," declares the Lord, "because they have called you an outcast, saying: 'It is Zion; no one cares for her.'" Jeremiah 30:16–17 (NAS)

There are many details in this passage that need expounding, but before we do, may we stand in awe, silent in sorrow, as God Himself does, at the enormity of Jewish suffering throughout the past two millennia. For only then will we be able to respond to God's cry, *"Comfort ye, comfort ye My people. Speak tenderly to the heart of Jerusalem that she has suffered double for all her sins."* (See Isaiah 40:1–2.)

In about A.D. 32, when Jesus was to be arrested and tried, He spoke the following words to His friends, the Jewish disciples:

"All of you will be made to stumble because of Me this night, for it is written: 'I will strike the Shepherd, and the sheep will be scattered.'" Mark 14:27

These words were very much like those spoken by the old Jewish prophet Simeon in the temple, when he held the baby Jesus in his trembling hands:

"Behold, this Child is destined for the fall and rising of many in Israel, and for a sign which will be spoken against." Luke 2:34

Jesus, when He had become a full-grown man, foresaw the terrible suffering that would come upon Jerusalem and wept over the city, lamenting:

> *"For the days will come upon you when your enemies will build an embankment around you, surround you and close you in on every side, and level you, and your children within you, to the ground; and they will not leave in you one stone upon another, because you did not know the time of your visitation."* Luke 19:43–44

To the Jewish women who accompanied Him on the *via dolorosa,* Jesus said,

> *"Daughters of Jerusalem, do not weep for Me, but weep for yourselves and for your children. For indeed the days are coming in which they will say, 'Blessed are the barren, the wombs that never bore, and the breasts which never nursed!' Then they will begin to say to the mountains, 'Fall on us!' and to the hills, 'Cover us!' For if they do these things in the green wood, what will be done in the dry?"* Luke 23:28–31

It is very much as the prophet Zechariah also foresaw, how after God's "Companion and Shepherd" would be smitten, a terrible time would descend upon His people. It is frightening the way these prophetic words all were fulfilled to the letter. Not one of the stones of the beautiful temple buildings that took Herod 43 years to complete remained upon another. Multiplied thousands of Israelites massed in the city—men, women and children—as they were surrounded by the Roman legions. After a siege which lasted many months, the soldiers broke into the city, slaughtering over 600,000 of the Jewish people. Later, in A.D. 73, at Masada, the Romans repeated their actions, leading the last resisting Jews to commit suicide, rather than fall into the hands of the Gentiles.

> *"And it shall come to pass in all the land,"* says the Lord, *"that two-thirds in it shall be cut off and die, but one-third shall be left in it: I will bring the one-third through the fire, will refine them as silver is refined, and test them as gold is tested."* Zechariah 13:8–9

This is exactly what happened, as related by the Jewish historian of the time, Josephus. Not only did the Jews massed inside Jerusalem die by the hundreds of thousands. Later, after Bar Kochba's rebellion, the Roman sword went once more "through the land," slaughtering so many Jews that the Mediterranean became red with the blood of God's people.

However, in no way can God's anger and disappointment with His people ever be used to justify the horrible crimes of anti-Semitism. These were perpetrated not only by Romans, but by the Crusaders, priests, monks and many other Christian clergy and laity, right through the centuries until the horrible days of the Holocaust. Not only the execution of all these millions of acts of cruelty and anti-Semitism, but also, the lack of compassion and the shortage of comforters among those who should have shown mercy is lamented and rebuked by God.

Though God states that He has His own case against the Jewish people, He is furious about the treatment the nations have heaped upon those He calls His own—as well as the Gentiles' almost total lack of mercy or love. He states that if He has not spared His own people, He certainly will not spare those who have committed these acts against His people. *"For the Lord has a day of vengeance, a year of recompense for the cause of Zion."* Isaiah cries out. Isaiah 34:8 (NAS)

In Jeremiah God says,

"And fear not, O Jacob My servant," declares the Lord, "and do not be dismayed, O Israel; for behold, I will save you from afar, and your offspring from the land of their captivity. And Jacob shall return, and shall be quiet and at ease, and no one shall make him afraid. For I am with you," declares the Lord, "to save you; for I will destroy completely all the nations where I have scattered you, only I will not destroy you completely. But I will chasten you justly...." Jeremiah 30:10–11 (NAS)

As God speaks through another prophet,

"Proclaim, saying, 'Thus says the Lord of hosts, I am exceedingly jealous for Jerusalem and Zion. But I am very angry with the nations who are at ease; for while I was only a little angry, they furthered the disaster.'" Zechariah 1:14–15 (NAS)

The full extent of the evil exacted against and suffered by the Jewish people we could never fathom. These few examples, though, help to reveal the depth and enormity of their agony through the ages. May they cause us to become comforters of God's people and fill us with tears of contrition about the way many Christians—who say they believe in a God of love and compassion—have failed so terribly in showing that love and compassion to the very ones God has referred to as "His chosen people."

Here is how William Hull describes that awful massacre by the Romans:

In Jerusalem, three factions were fighting among themselves for leadership in the defence and only stopped what had already become a bloody civil war when the Romans actually approached the city. Valiantly the Jews of Jerusalem met the Roman attack which was commanded by Titus, the son of Vespasian (who in the meantime had returned to Rome and been crowned emperor). The city had three walls, one inside the other, and successively they fell until only the Temple area was left to the Jews. On the ninth of Av, three weeks after the last available animal had been offered as the Temple sacrifice, the Romans attacked and succeeded in burning the main gate and entering the Temple area.

Then began one of the most horrible slaughters in history, as the Jews fought to the death or threw themselves into the flames of the burning Temple. Before the Temple fire was well advanced Titus personally forced his way into the Holy of Holies, and for the last time this sacred spot was defiled, even as the flames licked at the walls. Never again was a Jewish sacrifice to be offered to God on the altar in Jerusalem. The Law demanded a sacrifice, yet God who had made the Law permitted His Temple and altar to be destroyed in spite of every expectation of the Jews that it would be miraculously delivered. God demanded a sacrifice for justification from sin, and then allowed the means to be taken away. Is God unjust? Could it be that because He had already provided His Son as a perfect sacrifice according to His promise, this very perfection replaced all former imperfect sacrifices and did away with the need of any future sacrifice? It was in this same city, only forty years earlier, that One who had been called the Lamb of God had died. He had died facing the very Temple that Israel later mourned for through the centuries. And as He died He cried, "Father, forgive them! for they know not what they do."

With the destruction of the Temple many of the Jews who survived were scattered to other lands, many of them sold as slaves. *Their exile had begun.* Once more, in 132 A.D., under Bar Kochba (whom some believed to be the Messiah), the remnant of the Jews in Judea gathered in rebellion against the power of Rome. In 135 A.D., they made a stand at Bethar, a city probably near Jerusalem, but their defeat there by the Roman armies finally resulted in the overthrow of all Jewish resistance. Five hundred and eighty thousand Jews were said to have been killed in battle and the slave markets were glutted with Jewish captives. Judea was now all but empty of Jews.(124)

In a popularized version of Josephus' history, Rabbi Leibel Reznick, in his moving booklet *Woe, Jerusalem,* writes,

Fire still raged in the Temple courtyard. The Zealots had fled to the Upper and Lower Cities, the only protected sections of the Holy City that remained. The Romans brought their standards and flags into the Temple grounds and posted them near the eastern gate. The legionnaires still encamped on the Mount of Olives, across from the eastern gate, watched with relief and pride.

The Romans raided the Temple treasuries, which were so laden with precious metals that the price of gold soon dropped by one half throughout the Middle East. Some priests were found still hiding in the Temple grounds. They were brought before Titus and executed.

The last remaining wall of the City began at the southeastern corner of the Temple. It went southward, following the contour of the Kidron Valley. It then turned west as far as the Valley of Hennom. From there it began its northern course to the tower of David. From the fortress it turned to the east and went across the mountain where the Upper City was located. The wall crossed the mountain and then across the Tyropean Valley until it joined the western Temple wall. This area was the last secure confine of Jerusalem.

The surviving revolutionaries and citizens were crowded into this district. Titus stood atop the western Temple wall and addressed Yochanan and Shimon and their revolutionary cohorts standing below. "The leaders of the rebellion must surrender. They will be justly punished but their followers will be granted immunity." Yochanan demanded that they all be granted a safe passage out of the wartorn city, into the Judean hills. Titus was appalled that the Zealots tried to impose demands as though they were the victors instead of prisoners. Titus ordered his troops to devastate the city.

Before this dreadful war, this very day, the Fifteenth of Av, was a holiday. It was a day of celebration. The cutting of the trees for the Temple firewood had been completed. Maidens would dance in the vineyards in all their linen finery. They would all borrow and lend clothing to one another in order not to embarrass those who did not have the proper garments. Matchmakers would make matches, and not long after, the music of betrothal celebrations would fill the land. But now there was no dancing. There was no celebration.

There was no music. The Temple had been destroyed. Judea had been made desolate. The survivors of the Jewish nation were surrounded in the last remaining corner of Jerusalem. The day was no longer a day of feasts and gaiety; it was a day of mourning and despair.(125)

But the terrible tale of suffering continued right through the Middle Ages, culminating in the unbelievable agony of the twentieth-century Holocaust.

As Dr. Michael Brown writes in his deeply moving book about the tragic story of the "Church" and the Jewish people,

True love afflicts the heart.... Jesus wept when He saw the dark future of His people.... [F]or almost 2000 years now, each day has had its share of pain. Concentration camp survivor and Nazi hunter Simon Wiesenthal has compiled a chronicle of Jewish martyrdom for every day of the year. Here is merely *one typical day,* selected at random from Wiesenthal's chronicle, in the agonizing history of our people.(126) All these tragedies occurred on June 23, one day out of many in our people's saga of sorrow:

1270 In Weissenburg, Germany, 7 Jews are arrested without charges held against them, tortured, and executed.

1298 The Rindfleisch Persecutions... annihilated 146 Jewish communities in southern and central Germany.

In Windsheim in Franconia 55 Jews are burned at the stake; 900 Jews of the large community of Wurzburg are slain, among them 100 who had sought refuge there from other places. In the little town of Neustadt on the Aisch River, 71 Jews are burned to death.

1475 In the case of Simon of Trent (Italy), a Christian child is found dead and Samuel, a wealthy Jew, and others of his brethren are falsely accused and subjected to torture. The boy is proclaimed a martyr and the Jews are kept imprisoned and tortured from March to April. On June 23, Samuel is burned at the stake and the others burned or broken on the wheel. Simon of Trent is venerated as a martyr until the intervention of the Vatican in 1965.

1919 During a pogrom, 45 Jews are slaughtered, many are severely wounded, and 35 Jewish women are raped by [army] insurgents… in Skvira, Kiev.

1941 After the Germans invade Sokal, Poland [today Ukraine], where 6,000 Jews live, 8 Jews are shot….

1942 The SS murders 850 Jews in Wielopole, in the district of Cracow, Poland. The first selection for the gas chambers in the Auschwitz extermination camp in Poland takes place on the platform of the train arriving from Paris, France….

1943 A deportation train leaves Paris for Auschwitz, carrying 1,000 Jews, among them 100 children under the age of 16 and 13 babies, who are all killed upon arrival. All inmates of the Jewish home for the aged of Moravska Ostrava, Czechoslovakia, are deported to Auschwitz…. A deportation train with 1,018 Jewish people leaves from the Drancy transit camp in the German occupied zone of France for Auschwitz. On their arrival, 518 are gassed; 72 men and 37 women will survive.(127)

The Holocaust, after all the suffering the Jewish people had already endured throughout the dispersion since Titus, was by far the worst. It was the time of Jacob's trouble, unequaled in terror and severity, as Jeremiah had predicted—a day so terrible *that there was none like it* in Jewish history.

Elie Wiesel, himself a Holocaust survivor, wrote about this dreadful event in a book he called—not without cause—*Night*. In it he writes the following:

> I witnessed other hangings. I never saw a single one of the victims weep. For a long time those dried-up bodies had forgotten the bitter taste of tears.

> Except once. The *Oberkapo* of the fifty-second cable unit was a Dutchman, a giant, well over six feet. Seven hundred prisoners worked under his orders, and they all loved him like a brother. No one had ever received a blow at his hands, nor an insult from his lips. He had a young boy under him, *apipel,* as they were called—a child with a refined and beautiful face, unheard of in this camp.... (The Dutchman's little servant was loved by all. He had the face of a sad angel.)

> One day, the electric power station at Buna was blown up. The Gestapo, summoned to the spot, suspected sabotage. They found a trail. It eventually led to the Dutch Oberkapo. And there, after a search, they found an important stock of arms.

> The Oberkapo was arrested immediately. He was tortured for a period of weeks, but in vain. He would not give a single name. He was transferred to Auschwitz. We never heard of him again.

> But his little servant had been left behind in the camp in prison. Also put to torture, he too would not speak. Then the SS sentenced him to death, with two other prisoners who had been discovered with arms.

One day when we came back from work, we saw three gallows rearing up in the assembly place, three black crows. Roll call. SS all round us, machine guns trained: the traditional ceremony. Three victims in chains—and one of them, the little servant, the sad-eyed angel.

The SS seemed more preoccupied, more disturbed than usual. To hang a young boy in front of thousands of spectators was no light matter. The head of the camp read the verdict. All eyes were on the child. He was lividly pale, almost calm, biting his lips. The gallows threw its shadow over him.

This time the *Lagerkapo* refused to act as executioner. Three SS replaced him.

The three victims mounted together onto the chairs.

The three necks were placed at the same moment within the nooses.

"Long live liberty!" cried the two adults.

But the child was silent.

"Where is God? Where is He?" someone behind me asked.

At a sign from the head of the camp, the three chairs tipped over.

Total silence throughout the camp.

On the horizon, the sun was setting.

"Bare your heads!" yelled the head of the camp. His voice was raucous. We were weeping.

"Cover your heads!"

Then the march past began. The two adults were no longer alive. Their tongues hung swollen, blue-tinged. The third rope was still moving; being so light, the child was still alive.... For more than half an hour he stayed there, struggling between life and death, dying in slow agony under our eyes. And we had to look him full in the face. He was still alive when I passed in front of him. His tongue was still red, his eyes were not yet glazed.

Behind me, I heard the same man asking:

"Where is God now?"

And I heard a voice within me answer him:

Where is He? Here He is—He is hanging here on this gallows....

That night the soup tasted of corpses.(128)

Maybe one of the most intensely shocking books on the Holocaust, one that should be read by all who wish to feel at least some of the pain of the Jewish people, is written about Elli—a very young girl who went through the Holocaust together with her mother.(129)

One reviewer writes, "How can one critic tell you that amidst the glut of books being produced these days, amidst the wave of books by Holocaust survivors, there is one book, this one, which overshadows all but a few" (West Coast Review of Books).

Elli recounts,

I am terribly hungry. This is the fifth day of Passover. Mummy and I had decided that one of us would observe Passover by not eating the bread ration and the other one would compensate for the bread by sharing her ration of the cooked meals at noon and in the evening. I had volunteered to give up the bread ration. Mummy had agreed because she was in far worse physical shape than I. So I had only black coffee in the morning, and one and a half bowls of soup at noon and in the evenings. All that liquid without the morning and evening ration of bread made me ravenously hungry, and by the third day I felt quite weak. Now, on the fifth day, having forgone the coffee in the morning, I am feeling faint. I find it difficult to stand, but I am afraid to crouch even when the Germans are not looking. I do not dare attempt a second violation in one day.

So I stand alongside the wall among the others. In a couple of hours we are all sorely fatigued and our campmates cast compassionate glances at us. They are not permitted to speak to us. Poor Mummy keeps walking back and forth, passing me every few minutes, her face a mask of pity. I make an effort to encourage her but as the hours pass, it proves increasingly difficult.

The cauldron of soup is distributed in the hall right before our noses. So is the evening meal and bread. But we stand there and believe the day will never end. My legs feel wooden and the length of my spine is a stripe of pain. My stomach feels heavy and numb. There is a light trembling in my whole body. I am very cold.

At 10 p.m., after the camp had gone to bed, the *Oberscharführer* comes to us.

"Are you tired? Are you hungry? Did you learn your lesson?"

We begin to cry. We are beyond fatigue. Beyond hunger.

"Go to your blocks!"

We are barely able to move. Slowly, we trudge to our respective rooms.

In my room it is dark and quiet. Noiselessly, I approach my bed. Mummy stirs. She sits up abruptly and embraces me: "Thank God, it's over! Come, sit here for a moment." From under her blanket she takes out a bowl of cold soup. It is her supper. She has been saving it for me.

"Eat it, you must be faint with hunger."

"It is your supper. You have not eaten from it. I will eat half. Take out your spoon and let's eat together."

"No, I'll not eat. You have to eat it all, you have not eaten all day."

"Look, Mummy. I am very hungry, it is true. And I will eat half of the soup. But you must eat the other half because you have become very weak and thin and every drop of food you deny yourself may prove disastrous. Take your spoon and let's eat together."

Mother gets very angry. She whispers: "Stop talking and eat!"

She takes the spoon and thrusts it into the soup. Then raises it to my mouth.

I shake my head with lips shut tight. Mummy looks at me, her face aflame. But I am adamant.

"I will not eat if you will not share it with me."

Mummy's anger and despair charge the air. "If you will not eat the soup I will empty the bowl on top of the bed!"

I shake my head. "I will eat only if you will also eat."

Mummy takes the bowl of soup and turns it over. In a splash, the contents land on top of her grey blanket. Pieces of potato scatter in every direction. The liquid is being sucked up by the bedding.

I cannot believe my eyes.

The soup. There is no soup! Mummy has deliberately spilled it, and on the bed! Oh, my God, what has happened? What has happened to her? My God, what is happening to us?

"Mummy, why did you do this? For God's sake, why did you do it?!"

Mummy begins to cry. She hugs me and we lie down on my side of the narrow bed. I begin to cry, too. For the soup, for Mummy, for all the unhappy, miserable, cold, and hungry prisoners of the world.

We cried until dawn. Our weeping was uncomforting, heavy and hopeless. Bitterness burned my throat. Unrelieved, oppressive, desperate. The sky seemed to darken with the coming of dawn. Our grief was total, and for the first time, uncontrollable.

Much later we found that was the night Daddy died— on the fifth day of Passover.(130)

The following story comes out of the concentration camp, Treblinka:

Pain—and consciousness—returned only at the end of a month after the Technicians had begun to reorganize the camp. At that time there were fifteen hundred prisoners in Treblinka. Many committed suicide, either with poison found in the baggage of those who were gassed, or by hanging themselves at night in the barracks. The conditions made hanging very difficult, and many struggled for a long time before they were still. Later, when the beginnings of social life began to establish itself among the prisoners, the technique improved. You had a friend pull the box away; indeed, this became the greatest proof of friendship. The desperate man would get up on a box, put his belt around his neck and attach it to a beam. When everything was ready, he would say, "Now!" The friend would quickly pull the box away and then recite a prayer. When two friends were very close and both wanted to end it, they drew straws and the loser, after pulling the box away, would either have to hang himself or look for another friend.

It was a father and son who had been the first to utilize this method. The son was still a young boy, the father already an old man. They were the last remnants of a large family. The father had urged the son to live in order to perpetuate their name, but now the son was a clepsydra (a prison inmate sentenced, or marked for death). When his son had asked him whether he was marked, at first the father had not dared to answer. The murmur of their discussion had lasted long into the night in the barracks.

"Tell me, Father, tell me frankly," asked the son.

"No, my son, there's nothing there," answered the father, running his hand over his son's face. "You will live, and you will perpetuate our name."

So powerful was the father's desire to have his lineage survive that he was ready to take the risk of having his son die in great agony.

"You will live, and you will go to the land of Israel, our land, you will marry and raise children, my children, the children of my father and my father's father. You will teach them our religion and the fear of God. You will also tell them how we died, so that the world will never forget it. You will make our land an impregnable citadel, which will fear the Lord, blessed be His Name, and be feared by its enemies."

The voice swelled like a prophecy.

"Yes, Father," answered the son timidly.

"And it shall come to pass that in all the land," said the Lord, "two parts therein shall be cut off and die, but the third shall be left therein. I will bring the third part through the fire, and will refine them as silver is refined, and will try them as gold is tried. They shall call on My Name and I will hear them. I will say: 'It is My people,' and they shall say, 'The Lord is my God!'"

"You will be among the third whom the prophet Zechariah foretells," said the father, "and I will be cut off. But you will be refined like silver and tried like gold. So the Lord decided, blessed be His Name."

"Father," said the child suddenly, "I'm afraid."

The father said nothing for a long time. When he began to speak again, his voice was changed, softer, sadder.

"You do not have confidence?" he asked.

"I'm afraid."

The voice of the child tried to be steady, but it shook a little.

"I felt blood on my fingers."

For a long time the father stroked the face of his son who would not go to the land of Israel, who would not have children, who was the last of his name, and who was going to die.

"God does not exist," murmured the child.

This blasphemy, uttered with a pure heart, did not disturb the father.

"Yes He does, my son," he answered in a voice full of love, "but we do not understand Him. Our sins have stopped our ears and closed our eyes."

"I'm afraid," said the son again. "They are going to kill me. I don't want them to kill me. I don't think I can stand it."

And he fell against his father, who held him in his arms for a long time, murmuring prayers. Finally, as if coming out of a deep meditation, the father said, "Come, my son, prepare to die."

"Yes, Father," answered the child with total submission.

The father took off his belt and knotted it around the child's neck. Then he made him stand on a box and climbed up beside him to fasten the belt to a beam. When this was done, he embraced his son and got down. "Goodbye," murmured the son. "Until later," answered the father, and he pulled the box away quickly.

After a few minutes he came back, climbed onto the box, and took down his son's body. He laid it gently on the sand floor of the barracks and began to recite a prayer.

Voices had risen in the barracks, hushed, anonymous and fraternal, swelling each open "Amen." But when the father put the belt around his own neck, no one made a move. He mounted the box, groped with raised arms to fasten the belt, then, with a sudden movement, kicked over the box. His body strained, shuddered, and was still. The funeral murmur resumed, profound as death, eternal as faith. That night marked the first sign of the rebirth of a social life among the Jews of Treblinka.(131) (Emphasis added.)

What seems so very, very sad is that the people Paul told to show compassion to the Jews, the Christian believers, failed so miserably in doing so during most of the Church's long history.

As Dennis Prager and Joseph Telushkin write,

Christianity did not create the Holocaust; indeed Nazism was anti-Christian, but it made it possible. Without Christian anti-semitism, the Holocaust would have been inconceivable.... Hitler and the Nazis found in medieval, Catholic, anti-Jewish legislation, a model for their own, and they read and reprinted Martin Luther's virulently anti-semitic writings. It is instructive that the Holocaust was unleashed by the only major country in Europe having approximately equal numbers of Catholics and Protestants. Both traditions were saturated with Jew-hatred.(132)

Michael Brown writes,

What happened to Christian love? Paul wished that he could be cursed in place of his Jewish people. Chrysostom instead cursed them! How much destruction was subsequently ignited by these tragic sermons of malice? The Catholic historian Malcolm Hay is surely right when he says: "For many centuries the Jews listened to the echo of those three words of St. John Chrysostom, the Golden-Mouthed: 'God hates you.'" And thus, the popular Christian doctrine has always been that anyone, whether pagan or Christian, who has at any time persecuted, tortured or massacred Jews, has acted as an instrument of divine wrath.(133)

During the long, dark years of the Middle Ages, Jews were frequendy given the option of baptism or expulsion, baptism or torture, baptism or death. Every type of degrading law was passed against them.(134)

The Bible spoke about this terrible valley of agony that the Jewish people would go through. Jeremiah saw it as the "time of Jacob's trouble," Ezekiel as the "valley of dry bones." But this horror would be immediately followed by a miraculous rebirth of the nation.

In other words, the generation that would see the holocaust would also see the subsequent return to the land God had promised them, heralding the greatest time yet to come for the Jewish people.

Listen to the words of these two prophets:

Alas! For that day is great, so that none is like it; and it is the time of Jacob's trouble, but he shall be saved out of it. "For it shall come to pass in that day," says the Lord of hosts, "that I will break his yoke from your neck, and will burst your bonds; foreigners shall no more enslave them. But they shall serve the Lord their God, and David their king, whom I will raise up for them. Therefore do not fear, O My servant Jacob," says the Lord, "nor be dismayed, O Israel; for behold, I will save you from afar, and your seed from the land of their captivity. Jacob shall return." Jeremiah 30:7–10

The hand of the Lord was upon me, and He brought me out by the Spirit of the Lord and set me down in the middle of the valley; and it was full of bones... and behold there were very many on the surface of the valley; and lo, they were very dry...Then He said to me, "Son of man, these bones are the whole house of Israel; behold, they say, 'Our bones are dried up, and our hope has perished. We are completely cut off.' Therefore prophesy, and say to them, Thus says the Lord God, "Behold, I will open your graves and cause you to come up out of your graves, My people; and I will bring you into the land of Israel." Ezekiel 37:1–2, 11–12 (NAS)

Notice that in both of these passages, the return of the Jews to their land is preceded by this terrible, cataclysmic event that the prophets foresee.

It is as Mr. Menachem Begin, former prime minister of Israel, told 5,000 Holocaust survivors assembled at Jerusalem's Western Wall in 1981:

> My dear people, let us not forget that we, the generation who saw the darkest page of Jewish history—the Holocaust—also saw the brightest. It was this generation that saw the rebirth of the State of Israel and the reuniting of our capital Jerusalem!

If, however, the question is asked whether it was necessary for such a terrible tragedy to precede such a wonderful—biblically prophesied—event as the rebirth of Israel, the answer must be an emphatic "No"!

Many Jewish people simply cannot believe in God and His love anymore after the terrible experience of the Holocaust. Elie Wiesel, a Holocaust survivor, has faced this terrible, internal battle. Though he certainly cannot be described as an irreligious man, he has a deep struggle in his heart with God. I met him briefly after a profoundly moving speech during which one could feel the pain and question of his heart. I felt a need to answer this cry which I had sensed, and later wrote to him:

> Once more I want to thank you for the wonderful words you spoke yesterday evening, and also for the kindness with which you were willing to converse with me afterwards. I myself am a speaker and know how people can press in upon one after a meeting, and I appreciated your nonprofessional, warm, personal approach.

I hesitate in a way to write to you the things I will, for the matters you touched upon in your speech are so deep and so holy that any reply to them seems to be cheap or out of place. Nevertheless because of my respect for you, I venture to reply as to a friend, wanting nothing but the very best for you. Probably it would be better to converse with you face to face to help one another further as we think aloud, but I would hardly dare to make such a demand upon your precious time. Therefore a letter.

My wife and I live in Jerusalem, in Israel. I have two children and my son is serving in "your" Israeli Army, if I may put it like this. I am spokesman for the International Christian Embassy Jerusalem which wants to be a beacon of comfort and practical help to the people of Israel! This includes a branch for the Soviet Jewry and our concern generally for the Jewish people. We opened the Embassy as a response to the exodus of thirteen embassies out of Jerusalem in 1980, after the Jerusalem Law was passed in the Israeli Knesset.

We are trying worldwide to be a voice that speaks up for Israel, and are thankful to be able to do this. What we really do is what Ruth the Moabitess did when she said to Naomi, "Let your God be my God and your people be my people. Where you lie down, there I will lie down, where you go, I will go and where you die, I will die."

We love Israel and the people of Israel and believe that they are the great sign of God's goodness; that He has not only not forgotten His people but through them not forgotten His world.

You spoke as a Jew carrying the concern for this bleeding world in a way that deeply spoke to me and convicted me. Of course with all my heart I wish you would already live with us and your people in Israel.

I remember how Mr. Begin spoke some years ago at the Western Wall, the same evening that you spoke for the

5,000 Holocaust survivors and asked them this question, "My people, where was our God when six million of our people were brutally murdered?" I still remember his answer, he said, "If it had not been for the mercy of the Lord that left us a remnant to see this day of our redemption, we would have all been like Sodom and Gomorrah, and let us not forget that our generation that saw the darkest page in our history also saw the brightest page, the return to Eretz Israel and Jerusalem. It is this generation that saw a returned Jerusalem."

The Jewish faith is universal, but not without a center. It has a geographical focus point and that is Jerusalem. When I see the Isaiah Wall before the UN building, on which are written the words, "Then shall the nations turn their swords into ploughshares and teach war no longer," I know that your prophet did not see this vision coming true through the efforts of that organization of the nations, called the UN, but saw this come to pass as a result of the Jews returning to their land and city of Jerusalem. Not New York, New York, if I forget thee let my right hand forget her cunning, but Jerusalem is the only city where this prophecy will one day be fulfilled, and in that day all the nations including the leaders of the United Nations will go up to Jerusalem. I firmly believe this and in this spirit I pray fervently for the peace of Jerusalem, for in her destiny lies the destiny of the world.

Wherever your people, marked as chosen by God to be a light to the nations, have wanted to carry that burden to change this world or help it to become more humane, they have principally failed. This world is not going to be changed by your people living in Boston, Berkeley, California, Moscow or Germany among the Gentiles. That is the tragedy of Marx, Freud, Einstein and many others. A Jew has to pay a price to change this world, he has to make aliya, he has to go up to Jerusalem, to Israel. It is from there that he was meant to be a blessing and a light to all the peoples of the world.

It is amusing to me to see how Jerusalem has even in the political world only become the focal point of attention, not when it was in British hands nor when it was in Turkish hands or in Jordanian hands, but when it returned to Jewish hands.

Sometimes I have been asked over the many years that I have lived in Jerusalem, "where was God when the Holocaust occurred?" It is a terrible question and may be as you said, more terrible to try to answer. But then by not answering it, the One who pays the bill is God. The very One I am meant to love with all my heart, is left in the unholy position of being accused of failing to live up to be the One He claimed to be, a merciful Father. So not to answer is making Him pay. He will be doubted. He will be accused. He who suffered more with and for His people during all these years, more than can even be imagined or expressed. Does He need to be punished? You expressed it so beautifully in your speech when you said that in the beginning it was not man questioning God but God putting His question to man, "Where are you?" I loved this point you made, I dislike man's arrogance always giving himself the right to question God, without being willing to be exposed to God questioning Him.

The book of Job is one of the most poignant examples of this. First there are the cheap, religious, neatly cut answers by his friends, which do not satisfy either Job or God, so that in the end Job has to pray for his religious self-assured friends. Then comes Job's near-rebellious questioning of God right through the book, and finally God answers Job, as you said in your speech, by questioning Job. It is only then that the righteous Job, a *tsadik* (righteous one), says, "I abhor myself and repent in dust and ashes."

It is a pity how we who claim to believe the Book of Books, often conveniently interpret that book to fit our own outlook and philosophy. God saw the monstrous power of prejudice and anti-Semitism coming up like a cloud in the hearts and minds of many Europeans in the beginning of this century. And in His love and mercy for His people, began to work for His people in preparing them a way of escape which was Israel. He touched the heart of Theodor Herzl, who wrote, "We Jews have not yet sufficiently been trampled upon to believe that our only hope is to return to Zion." Jabotinsky said to thousands upon thousands, "liquidate the diaspora or the diaspora will liquidate you." However His people, that God through all these men wanted to save, did not want to leave the fleshpots of Europe in accord with God's own promise: "And I will gather you from the nations where you have scattered and bring you back to the land of your fathers." He had even made it politically possible, not only by sending the Zionists but by putting it in the heart of Balfour to officially open up the land of Palestine for Jewish immigration.

However Jabotinsky died as a pauper in New York. Theodor Herzl felt so rejected that he wrote in his diary, "I have the right to become the world's greatest anti-Semite," and he died an early death.

The people that had laughed about these messengers of God's love, pleading with them to go up to Zion, died in the Holocaust. Your God, who warned your people of the invasion of Nebuchadnezzar through Jeremiah; of the Roman Holocaust by Titus through Jesus; and of the horrible, horrible liquidation by Hitler through the fiery Zionists, and opened the door of escape through Balfour, is nevertheless still questioned!

Dear Mr. Wiesel, I am a Gentile who believes with all my heart in what you Jews have taught about our God. I believe it is you and your people that He wants to bring home to Israel, to bring then this world home to Himself, when He will be King over all the world in Jerusalem. I live and pray earnestly for this day. I believe that in the end the quickest way to be involved with the redemption of this world is not by trying to be wiser than God, but by praying for the peace of Jerusalem. It is only from this city that one day all killing and injustice among the nations will stop.

You can try to save situations, individuals, even groups of people from Boston, from injustice, from oppression, from death, but when they have been saved, in what kind of nations will they grow up, what kind of people will they become, how will they live? Will they use their gained freedom from oppression to oppress others? Will they who suffered injustice now become unjust and harmful and egocentric themselves?

This world is not helped just by fighting for all the rights of men. It will only become a peaceful paradise of justice under the rightful reign of the Lord and that through His people in Jerusalem. After all the suffering you have gone through, you still prefer New York to Jerusalem. I wonder why, as a Gentile who lives with burning faith in your city's and people's destiny in Jerusalem.

What will bring the Jews home, to become then channels of blessing to the world? New outbursts of anti-Semitism? If you were in God's place—all loving and caring—wanting to bring the Jews of America and other nations home to heal this sad, torn world, how would you go about it?

You have a golden mouth, the hand of God is upon you. How would you go about convincing your Jewish people to come home? Will you be successful after all the sufferings they experienced in their history, after all the

promises of God to bring them back to the land of their
fathers, after all the centuries of praying at Seder night,
"LaShana haba'a b'Yerushalayim?" With all these biblical
incentives in your hand, with your enormous gifts, would
you as God's instrument be successful in bringing them
to understand that this world will never become again the
place it was created to be—without the Jews coming up
to Jerusalem to present themselves as a nation to God
for Him to heal the world through.

Do we force anti-Semitism, as horrible as it is, upon us as
the only way through which God is able to convince us?
I hope not.

Please forgive me if in any way my writing has been too
didactic, it is certainly not because I lack respect for you,
rather the opposite, because I found in you a man to
whom I believe I could entrust these thoughts.

With much respect and friendship.

Had the Jewish people believed the modern Zionist prophets
like Ze'ev Jabotinsky, Max Nordau and Theodor Herzl, who warned
them to flee from Europe and return to Eretz Israel, their land, none
of them would have died in the Holocaust.

*The only country in the region which Hitler or the Axis powers
were never able to touch was Palestine.* Hitler's forces came up to
Alamein near Alexandria in Egypt and up to the Balkans, but they
were never able to enter the Holy Land. This land was, during the
Second World War, one of the safest places of refuge. Had they
listened to the cry of the Zionists and seen the signs of the modern
Cyrus, Lord Balfour—who by his declaration opened the door to
allow the Jews to settle in Eretz Israel and to establish there a
national home—and had they gone there, the Jews would not have
died under the Nazis in Europe.

Wallenberg Balfour

Shaftesbury Wingate

Chapter Nine

Early Christian Zionists

I have attempted to truthfully relate just some of the terrible failures of the Christian Church through the centuries with regard to the Jewish people. It would be good at this point to mention some of those Christians who held beliefs sincere and deep enough to take the Scriptures seriously. They knew that without the Jews' return to Israel—the country God promised them as an everlasting possession—there would be no final redemption for this planet, Earth.

These Christians were found on mainland Europe, in Britain, in the United States and elsewhere. They firmly believed that it was the will of God for the Jewish people to return to their land, and they were willing to be instruments in God's hand to see this accomplished. They were, in that sense, the early Christian Zionists: men like Reverend William Hechler, friend of Dr. Theodor Herzl; Lord Shaftesbury, one of those who influenced Lord Balfour; Captain Orde Wingate, who helped form the Jewish Hagana defense force in the early stages; the Dutch ten Boom family; Raoul Wallenberg; and many others. Frans Kobler, in his book *The Vision Was There*, names many of them, as does Michael Prager in *Faith and Fulfillment*.

Even the Jewish English historian, Leonard Stein, admitted in his book *The Balfour Declaration*,

> The real force behind the movement for the restoration of the Jews to Palestine was the "religion party"…a body of devout and high-minded English Christians who, looking at the ferment in the East, believed that the time was at hand for the fulfillment of prophecy by the return of the Chosen People to the Holy Land, and that it was God's will that the British nation should be His instrument for achieving His purpose.(135)

Claude Duvernoy, a French theologian living in Israel, wrote in *The Prince and the Prophet*, concerning Palmerston, the British prime minister,

> Palmerston did not trifle with the Bible. One of his intimate friends, Lord Shaftesbury (himself deeply influenced by the famous "Zionist" pastor Mac-Caul), had no difficulty in persuading him that messianic times were ripening for Israel: Great Britain…should seize this unique opportunity to follow the divine will that leads history. "And I will bless them that bless thee." Shaftesbury reminded his friend, the Prime Minister, that the promise given to all of Abraham's friends (Genesis 12:3) still remained valid.(136)

Palmerston, in turn, on January 22, 1839, was inspired to write to the British queen the following words:

> May it be during your reign that, according to the hope of this unique people now laid before your Majesty, "Judah shall be saved and Israel shall dwell in peace."(137)

The memorandum Palmerston enclosed was the one the General Assembly of the Church of Scotland, after having sent a committee of investigation to Palestine, had forwarded to the European monarchs, which said, *inter alia,*

> ...on the matter of the Restoration of the Jewish people in the land of Palestine...we are convinced of the truth of that divine promise which wills that a heavenly blessing repose upon those who come to the aid of the People of God, at present in affliction....(138)

Even in the United States there were many such Christians, as Duvernoy writes,

> In the United States, where the Puritan trend is powerful, the penchant for Zionism appeared in an American manner; that is practically, and in the form of petitions. The second President set the example: "I sincerely wish to see the Jews settled again in Judah, forming an independent nation," John Adams declared. At the end of the last century a petition was presented to President Harrison, on behalf of the "Conference for Christians and Jews," which requested of the Berlin Congress "a second Edict of Cyrus."(139)

The president of this organization for Christians and Jews was W.E. Blackstone, a jurist and theologian.

> The Jews have never abandoned this land of their own will, and they have not signed any treaty of capitulation, but they have succumbed in a desperate battle before the crushing power of Rome...they were sold as slaves.... Since then, having neither sovereign nor political representation, they are reclaiming their motherland by their writings, their faith and their prayers.... The violence by which Israel was kept out of its land, without means of appeal, is in principle equivalent to a continual conflict...no entreaty can change this situation until Israel will have the opportunity to present its demands before the one and only competent Authority, and International Conference.

Thus the Zionist Protestant movement, solidly installed in the lands of the Reformation, readily seeks to express itself on the political level, and will spread to other European countries.

In the first third of the XVIIth century, the Huguenot theologian, Zionist and humanist, Isaac de la Peyrere, introduced the Zionist idea into France, by an appeal to the king of France, having in view the return of the Jews to the promised land.(140)

Paul Grattan Guinness writes,

Prompted by humanitarian motives, Henri Dunant of Geneva, one of the founders of the World Alliance of Young Men's Christian Association (1855), and founder of the International Red Cross (1864), established a *Société Nationale Universelle pour le Renouvellement de l'Orient*, which in 1866 issued an appeal containing the suggestion that the rising Jewish colonies in Palestine might, like Switzerland, be diplomatically neutralized.

The publication in 1876 of George Eliot's *Daniel Deronda* was a landmark in Christian-Jewish Zionist aspirations. Addressed to the Jewish people, at the end of her long, creative literary career, *Daniel Deronda* reveals her conviction that the Restoration of the Jewish people is identical with their rebirth. She was convinced that: *The regeneration of the Jewish people is the great divine mystery of world history,* but the miracle must be wrought in Israel's soul.(141) (Emphasis in the original.)

In her biography of her uncle, Lord Balfour, Mrs. Blanche Dugdale writes,

His interest in the Jews and their history was lifelong. It originated in the Old Testament training of his mother, and in his Scottish upbringing. As he grew up, his intellectual admiration and sympathy for certain aspects of Jewish philosophy and culture grew also, and the problem of the Jews in the modern world seemed to him of immense importance. He always talked eagerly on this, and I remember in childhood imbibing from him the idea that Christian religion and civilisation owe an immeasurable debt to Judaism.

Balfour regarded human history much as Judaism does, as an instrument for carrying out a Divine purpose. He never forgot that first encounter with Weizmann. He came to realise that the Jewish form of patriotism was unique. The conversation convinced him that history could not thus be ignored and that if a home was to be found for the Jewish people, homeless now for nineteen centuries, it was vain to seek it anywhere but in Palestine.

He never wavered from this conviction, which led him to play the major role in bringing about the Balfour Declaration. His steadfastness was borne out by his statement to a Zionist delegation in Washington in January 1922:

"Where I stood in 1917, I stand now. The hope I entertained then I entertain still. The ideals for which I strove then are my ideals at this moment. My interest in the cause, my belief in its final success, my intense desire to see the ideal of the Jewish Home transformed into a great reality have not diminished or suffered any cooling during the years that have elapsed since the original Declaration was made."(142)

Another Christian Zionist was Laurence Oliphant, who "foresaw" the fate awaiting European Jewry. He was convinced assimilated Jews would face a crisis, and this was the driving force behind his appeal for the colonization of Palestine to save the Jewish people.

But maybe one of the foremost Christian Zionists was the aforementioned William Hechler, friend of the founder of the modern state
of Israel, Dr. Theodor Herzl. It was Hechler who, through his own
contacts with the Grand Duke Frederick of Baden, was able to intro-
duce both the idea of Zionism and its proponent, Dr. Herzl, to the
German Kaiser Wilhelm. Mrs. Hanna Bodenheimer, daughter of the
famous German Jew and Zionist leader, Dr. Max Bodenheimer, in a
welcoming word to the Christian Zionist Congress in Jerusalem in
1988 wrote,

> Hechler was the driving force that brought Herzl to the
> Court of the Grand Duke Frederick in Karlstruhe. Together
> with the Grand Duke they planned a meeting of Herzl and
> the German Kaiser. *Herzl's meeting with the Kaiser was*
> *decisive for the beginnings of political Zionism.* (At that
> time the Kaiser was the most powerful ruler in the world
> and the Turkish empire was in a state of dissolution.)
> Influenced by Hechler, the Grand Duke of Baden also
> became an ardent Christian Zionist. When the Grand Duke
> asked Hechler what he could do for the cause, Hechler
> answered that since the Grand Duke had proclaimed King
> Wilhelm of Prussia, German Emperor—the Grand Duke
> would participate in the restoration of the State of Israel.
> An example of Hechler's persistent lifelong dream is the
> following, written to the Grand Duke on his 70th birth-
> day: "According to the Bible the Jews must return to Pal-
> estine, and I therefore help this movement as a Christian
> and in complete faith for the truth of the Bible. For this is
> the cause of God."(143) (Emphasis added.)

In Holland, too, there were ardent lovers of the Jewish people.
It was Holland that had opened up its doors for the Jews after
they were expelled from Spain and Portugal, and in what appears
strangely appropriate—as God promises to bless those who bless
His people—Holland soon afterward entered her golden age, with
her famous painters such as Rembrandt, Frans Hals, Steen and others.

Corrie ten Boom, now famous in Christian circles all over the world, came from such a Christian family. Her grandfather started a prayer meeting in their house in Barteljoris Street for the restoration of the Jewish people. It was this same house, in which the ten Boom family had prayed for the Jewish people for over 100 years, that 18 Dutch Jews found a "Hiding Place" during the German occupation of Holland.

Corrie, her father and sister were caught by the Nazis. The elderly Mr. ten Boom was imprisoned and died while incarcerated in Scheveningen. Corrie's sister died in the Ravensbrück concentration camp. But Corrie ten Boom came back alive to tell her story to the world. Of course, there were many such Christian families all over Europe who knew and loved the God of Israel and the Lord and, therefore, also His own people.

My first wife, Widad (who died in 1995)—an Arab woman—had been brought up to hate and despise the Jews. She was told never to have a Jewish girlfriend. Yet when she was young, she heard the Spirit of God speak to her heart, "You cannot love Me and hate My people."

It was a bolt from the blue, completely against the mentality of her own upbringing, but she chose to obey her Lord and became one of the most courageous Christian Arabs, of any I have ever known, fighting to promote a loving attitude toward God's people, the Jews.

Sufficient has been said to at least demonstrate that alongside the appallingly shameful history of the Church's relationship to the Jewish people, there also were and are Christians who loved the Lord and who believed His Word enough to love His people, concerning whom the Scriptures say, *"...He who touches you touches the apple of His eye."* Zechariah 2:8

Ben Yehuda

Meir

Jabotinsky

Herzl

Nordau

Chapter Ten

The Jewish Zionists

*B*ut what about the Jewish Zionists? If the return of the Jews, as prophesied so many times throughout Scripture, was so important for God's purposes with this world, who were these men and women whom God, in His mercy and grace, used to bring about this modern-day miracle?

Those who presided over the miracle of the Jews returning home, the reclaiming of their barren, malaria-stricken land, the revival of their ancient Hebrew language—who were these people, and were they aware that they themselves were instruments in the hands of God for a greater purpose than even they could fathom?

Some of the most important of these heralders and founders of the Jewish State were Dr. Theodor Herzl—the founder of modern Zionism, Ze'ev Jabotinsky, Dr. Max Nordau, Eliezer Ben Yehuda—the author of modern Hebrew, Chaim Weizmann, David Ben Gurion, Golda Meir and Menachem Begin, to name but a few.

Theodor Herzl was born in Budapest in 1860. Years later, he became a journalist for one of Vienna's largest daily newspapers. Apparently, at that time, he did not realize he was divinely inspired and chosen by God to fulfill such an incredible destiny, yet he wrote the following amazing words in the beginning of his diary:

> I have been pounding away for some time at a work of tremendous magnitude. I do not know even now whether I will be able to carry it through. It bears the aspect of a mighty dream. For days and weeks it has saturated me to the limits of my consciousness; it goes with me everywhere, hovers behind my ordinary talk, peers at me over the shoulders of my funny little journalistic work, overwhelms and intoxicates me. What will come of it is still too early to say. However, I have had experience enough to tell me that even as a dream it is remarkable and should be written down—if not as a memorial for mankind, then for my own pleasure and meditation in years to come. The title: "The Promised Land."

Later on he wrote,

> During these days I have been more than once afraid that I was going mad. So wildly the streams of thought raced through my soul. A lifetime will not suffice to carry them out. But I am leaving behind me a legacy.(144)

To whom? To all men!

Even if Dr. Theodor Herzl was not a believing or orthodox Jew in any sense of the word, he nonetheless found himself being driven—compelled to write and act on behalf of the Jewish people and in that sense being an instrument in the purposes of God with His people.

This is true of most Jewish Zionists—they were not (in the strict sense) religious Jews. Yet they burned with a fire that drove them to speak in such a way about the need for the Jews of Europe to return to their Land that they at times even spoke prophetically.

"Liquidate the diaspora or the diaspora one day will liquidate you," warned Ze'ev Jabotinsky.

"One third of you shall be exterminated. One third of you shall be assimilated and one third of you shall be saved by returning to Palestine" were the words attributed to Dr. Max Nordau.

In his book about Theodor Herzl, Amos Elon relates how, shortly before Herzl died, he had told Reuben Brainin that when he was about 12 years of age the Messiah appeared to him in a dream:

> He took me in his arms and carried me off on the wings of Heaven. On one of the iridescent clouds we met Moses. His features resembled those of Michelangelo's statute. (As a child I loved this marble portrait.) The Messiah called out to Moses, "For this child I have prayed." To me He said, "Go and announce to the Jews that I shall soon come and perform great and wondrous deeds for My people and for all mankind." I have kept this dream to myself, and did not dare tell anyone.(145)

Prophetically inspired, Theodor Herzl wrote at the very end of his memorable book *Der Judenstaat* (The Jewish State) these words:

> Prayers will be offered up for the success of our work in temples and in churches also; for it will bring relief for an old burden, which all have suffered.(146)

Many of his Jewish contemporaries did not believe in the purity of his motives or vision. He was often spurned and maligned; nevertheless, sure of his vision—driven by a force outside himself—he continued, writing in his diary after the first Zionist Congress in Basel,

> "If I were to sum up the Basel Congress in one word—it would be this: At Basel I founded the Jewish State. If I were to say this today I would be met with universal laughter. In five years perhaps, and certainly in fifty, everyone will see it."(147)

Exactly 50 years after he had written these words, in 1948 in Tel Aviv, a white-haired David Ben Gurion proclaimed the birth of the new State of Israel.

A few years before Herzl died he had written, "God breaks the instruments that have served His purpose...no Moses ever enters the Promised Land.(148)

Dr. Max Nordau, one of the Zionist leaders present at that first Zionist Congress in the casino hall in Basel, said,

It seemed as if we were witnessing a miracle which affected ourselves, and all around us. We felt ourselves part and parcel of a fairytale, in which we saw our brethren, thousands of years buried, again become flesh and blood. We wanted, in the joy of this reunion, to rehearse the sad history of the hundreds of years in which we had been dead in our tombs.... .(149)

How reminiscent these words seem to be of the vision Ezekiel saw hundreds of years ago, when God said, *"Behold, O My people, I will open your graves and cause you to come up from your graves, and bring you into the land of Israel."* Ezekiel 37:12

Josef Fraenkel ends his biography on Theodor Herzl with the following beautiful words:

When Herzl was still hoping for success in El-Arish, he meant to migrate there—but no Moses ever reaches the promised land. After Egypt's stubborn refusal to grant Nile water, Herzl knew he would die outside and ordered a family vault in the Doebling cemetery in Vienna, where he should lie till the Jewish people could take his bones to Palestine. He appointed as executors of his last will, besides David Wolfsohn and Engineer Johann Kremenetsky, his London friend Joseph Coven.

When he died Zangwill wrote: "Not dead, because immortal," and he sent the following poem to Herd's newspaper, *Die Welt:*

Theodor Herzl
Farewell, oh Prince, farewell. Oh! sorely tried,
You dreamed a dream, and you have paid the cost:
To save a people leaders must be lost,
By friend and foe alike be crucified.
Yet, 'tis your body only that has died,
This noblest soul in Judah is not dust.

But fire that works in every vein—and must
Reshape our life, rekindling Israel's pride.
So we behold the captain of our strife:
Triumphant in this moment of eclipse:
Death has but fixed him in immortal life.
His flag upheld, the trumpet at his lips,
And while we, weeping, rend our garment's hem,
"Next year," we cry, "next year, Jerusalem."

At the edge of the grave of the creator of modern Zionism, David Wolfsohn repeated the oath taken by Herzl at the Zionist Congress: *"If I forget thee, Jerusalem, may my right hand wither."*

And at the Seventh Zionist Congress—the first Congress without Herzl—his successor declared, "I took this oath during our saddest hour of tribulation, beside Herzl's grave. I took it for you all, for all Zionists. We will repeat it, and always think of Jerusalem and never forget Zion, but never forget Herzl either.(150)

Perhaps one of the most remarkable Zionists was Ze'ev Jabotinsky, a high-class orator. He spoke several languages fluently, but could use about 15, and warned the Jews all over Europe and other parts of the world sometime before the Holocaust to go home.

There was much resentment in the Jewish communities against this fiery "preacher" and his message to return to Zion—many Jews were not yet ready for this message. But after the Holocaust, many of those who had survived knew that Jabotinsky, with his impassioned pleas, had been right—the only safe home for all Jews, in the end, was their own God-given land.

Colonel Patterson, an early Christian Zionist from Ireland, was a close friend of Ze'ev Jabotinsky and helped him organize a Jewish legion while they were together in Egypt. Patterson travelled at times with Jabotinsky, undergirding him in his vision and work with his deep, biblically based faith. Amazingly, just as William Hechler supported Theodor Herzl, Patterson was friend and encourager to Ze'ev Jabotinsky.

In Samuel Katz's extensive biography on Jabotinsky, the Zionist orator stands out as a warm-hearted, unselfish, deeply rooted family man with a great mind and a heart for his people in general and as individuals.

In his opening address at the founding conference of the New Zionist Organization, in autumn of 1935, Ze'ev Jabotinsky said,

> This matter (of the relationship between the Jewish State and Judaism) is exalting for the State, which for us is identical with the Nation; so that the perpetual flame be not extinguished; so that the voice of the Prophets continues to be heard as a living voice in the life of our society; so that there be preserved—amidst the confusion of the innumerable influences which engulf the youth in our days and oft-times lead them astray and contaminate them—the influence which is undoubtedly the purest of all, namely the spirit of the Lord.(151)

But even ordinary Jews, right through the centuries, were reminded in their prayers of this hope to one day return to Zion. Duvernoy writes,

> It is a moving experience to follow, through the (Jewish) prayer book of the Synagogue, Israel's yearning for Jerusalem and Zion.

> Ten times in the morning prayers alone, the pious Jew implores the Lord for the return to Zion, the rebuilding of the Temple and the promised land, and for final Redemption:

> "O cause us to return in peace from the four corners of the earth unto our own land, for the God that worketh salvation art Thou.... Rock of Israel, rise to the help of Israel and free, according to Thy promise, Judah and Israel!....

Cause the great trumpet to resound for our liberation, and the banner to be reared for the gathering of our exiles, and do Thou bring us together from the four corners of the globe. Blessed are Thou, O Lord, who gatherest and deliverest the scattered of Thy people Israel.... Blessed art Thou, O Lord who comfortest Zion and rebuildest Jerusalem...Let the scion of David, Thy servant, flourish speedily and enhance his power with Thy salvation.... Restore the service to the sanctuary of Thy House...."(152)

Who can be left unmoved by the longing expressed over the ages in this beautiful prayer and in the annually repeated prayer and wish made at each passover meal, all over the world, throughout all Jewish generations, "Lashana Haba'a b'Yerushalayim," (next year in Jerusalem)—repeated until they were virtually on the threshold of the gas chambers!

It is a prayer that God is now answering before our very eyes, in accordance with His own promise, that a day—"a set time to favor Zion"—would come, and that He would bring His people from their long and wide dispersion, from all the countries where they were scattered, back to their own land.

It is a prayer that Jews have prayed from the days of their captivity in Babylon until today, whenever they still find themselves in exile. It has the stamp of God's approval; not only has He always promised them that He would bring them home, but He has sanctified this longing by making it part of His own Word:

By the rivers of Babylon, there we sat down and wept, when we remembered Zion.. How can we sing the Lord's song in a foreign land? If I forget you, O Jerusalem, may my right hand forget her skill. May my tongue cleave to the roof of my mouth, if I do not remember you, if I do not exalt Jerusalem above my chief joy.
Psalms 137:1,4–6 (NAS)

The words by Peggy Mann about the young Golda Meir and her husband describe beautifully this intense feeling for Jerusalem.

> It was the spring of 1924. They moved to Jerusalem, the holy city in the Judean hills.... Since the age of five, when Shana had first told her about Zionism, this Passover prayer had taken on forceful meaning for Golda [Meir]. Now she was here, living in the city which had been the spiritual capital of the Jews for twenty centuries... Jerusalem.
>
> It held all the mystic beauty she had ever imagined. Especially at sunset. She and Morris would often walk together over one of the stony roads which stretched into the gaunt Judean hills, and they watched as the yellow limestone buildings reflected the glow of the sinking sun, and the city shimmered with a golden aura. Sometimes they stayed till the moon rose and the valleys brimmed deep with shadows, and the Past seemed to overtake the Present.(153)

It was this longing that kept Menachem Begin's heart beating—first while he suffered in the Dachau concentration camp, later when he was interrogated and tortured during the long and painful nights in the fortress of Lubianka, and then later still, in the Soviet concentration camp Pechorlag. Begin movingly describes how, in this awful hell of suffering and misery, he met a fellow prisoner named Garin, a man who had fallen from grace even though he was a communist and a former assistant editor of *Pravda:*

> In this atmosphere of stench and darkness, of suffering and maltreatment, of threats and horror, the crisis of the assistant editor of *Pravda,* who had fallen from the ruling heights to the realm of the *Urki* in the hold of a ship of hungry, sick, humiliated, wretched slaves, reached its climax. Garin was still suffering from the nights of interrogation in Tomsk, from the blows of the expert at

breaking stubborn cases, from his attempts on his own life. His suffering was increased by his expulsion from hospital, in spite of his temperature, in spite of his defective heart. And he suffered still more, every time he heard the word *"zhid"* spoken under the soviet sky, openly, insolently, with mocking scorn and hatred; unpunished, and without fear of punishment. This tortured man, the entire world of his dreams and his strivings crushed beneath the blows of reality, was no longer able to stand up to a new test, the test *of Etap.*

One day, Garin, who was lying some distance away from the Jewish prisoners, asked if he might lie next to me. My neighbour moved up a bit. We made room for him. Garin lay down beside me…. One day—it might have been night—Garin's voice aroused me from the semi-sleeping state that we were in perpetually, because of the dark, hunger, weakness, and the stench.

"Menachem! Menachem!" he called in a whisper.

It was the first time he had addressed me intimately, without adding my patronymic. "Do you remember the song '*Loshuv*'" He spoke to me in Yiddish for the first time.

"What song?" I asked, also in Yiddish. He had said *"Loshuv,"* and at first I did not understand him, perhaps because of his pronunciation, or perhaps because I was still half asleep.

"How is it that you don't know?" he asked rather crossly. "It's the song the Zionists sing, it's the song the Zionists used to sing in Odessa when I was still a boy. *Loshuv, Loshuv*—don't you know that song?"

"Ah! You mean *Hatikvah"* I said, using his pronunciation.

"Perhaps it is *Hatikvah.* What I remember is the word *Loshuv."*

"Yes, it is *Hatikvah*. You mean the song, *'Lashuv Le'Eretz Avotenu'* (the song of hope to return to the land of our fathers). Of course I remember it."...Together with Marmelstein I began to sing *Hatikvah*. Three other Jews, lying near us, joined in. We sang with the Ashkenazic pronunciation, the version in use in the lands of the dispersion. Garin listened in silence to the words: "To return to the land, the land of our fathers...."

The *Urki* woke up.

"What are the Jews singing there?"

"They're praying, they're praying to their God to help them."

Unruly laughter from the *Urki*.

We went on singing: "Harken my brothers in the lands of my wanderings...To return to the Land, the Land of our Fathers...."

The *Urki* were right. It was a prayer, not a song.

I felt as if I were saying the confessional prayer with a Jew who, like a kidnapped child, has pastured in strange fields and, on the threshold of death, after many tribulations returns to his people and his faith. Life does, indeed, create situations more fantastic than any in fiction. We are lying here, in the Valley of the Shadow of Death, among *Urki*, half-men, half-beasts. And with us lies Garin, former assistant editor of *Pravda*, a Communist from his earliest youth, estranged from his people, enemy of Zion, persecutor of Zionists. When last did he hear the strains of Hatikvah in Odessa? When last did he scoff at the *Loshuv?* What did he not do to destroy the "Hope to return"? What did he not do, what was he not ready to do, so that the other "hope" should be attained! Almost twenty-five years had passed since his life's dream had became a reality, since the triumph of the Revolution, for which he suffered, for which he was ready to give his life, for which he toiled and fought. Twenty-five years...and here was the reward of the Revolution to one to had been loyal to it, to one of its fighters, its leaders: traitor—enemy of humanity—spy—prison in Tomsk—expulsion from hospital—*"zhid"*—hauling iron—"zhid"—Etap—"zhid"—kicks—robbers—Urki—threats—entreaties to the robbers—card games—lice games—parasite—vermin—sick heart—fear—*"zhid"!* And when the time comes, after infinite trials and tribulations, what does the assistant editor of *Pravda,* General Secretary of the Ukrainian Communist Party, remind himself of? He reminds himself of *Loshuv.* "To return to the land of our fathers," that is his consolation.

And, perhaps for the first time since it began to flow northwards, the Pechora heard the prayer of confession and thanksgiving: "And out of the depths we cried unto the Lord: '*Lashuv Le'Eretz Avotenu* (Let us return to the land of our fathers).'"(154)

Chaim Weizmann's family, living against the background of pogroms and rioting against the Jews, veered into the movement "Lovers of Zion," which believed that the best country for the Jews to return to was the Land of Promise.

Chaim invariably returned home for the Passover, remaining for part of the summer, and that year, with sister Miriam and her family joining them, they were sixteen at the festive table. As always, Ozer conducted the Passover service, punctuated with songs, morality tales and humor, to make the *Seder,* as it was termed, an occasion for jollification, and hope, but never without a tinge of sorrow. When the herbs were brought in by the old family servant, they were eating the bread of affliction; when they broke the *matzo,* unleavened bread (and doubtless observed with deep distaste by the servant, for hadn't he, a gentile, been told that it was made with the blood of a Christian child?), it was the manna of hope, inspiring them all to chant "Next year in Jerusalem!"

Millions of Jews everywhere chanted the prayer as a mechanical rite. Not so the Weizmanns. Perhaps not next year literally, but even the youngest of them knew he was destined to exchange hated Russia and its oppressions for their real home, as He had promised. And as they relaxed at table news was exchanged of their acquaintances already settled in Palestine. Then the newspapers were passed around: *Hashiloach,* which came from Odessa and was edited by Ahad Ha'am, and *Hatzefira,* produced in Warsaw by the Hebrew journalist Nahum Sokolow, and then the Russian language *Voskhod.* The family read them for reports of a pogrom in a distant province, and for their stories from the colonies, and never an issue appeared but gave generous space to a speech by Ussishkin, and an account of the month's remittances sent off by the Lovers of Zion. If Kharkov or Minsk had suffered an exceptionally severe winter they would not have known of it. The periodicals told them of places in the Holy Land more familiar, and whether or not Jaffa had received adequate rain: a crop failure in Palestine was felt as a personal loss.(155)

The Bible prophesied that God would restore a pure language to His people as one of the many miracles of their restoration. (See Zephaniah 3:9.)

One day I, together with my father, met one of the daughters of the great Eliezer Ben Yehuda, the father of the modern Hebrew language.

She told us that her father had been inspired as though he had heard a voice from Heaven deep within his soul, telling him that he should set out to restore the ancient Hebrew language to His people.

Even though he had been very frail in health—under attack by tuberculosis—he set out, with incredible perseverance and endurance, to accomplish this enormous life task and, by the grace of God, succeeded.

As Eliezer Ben Yehuda was not an orthodox or religious Jew, his family never gave too much religious significance to the task and mission he had set out to accomplish for his people. Nevertheless, toward the latter part of his life, Eliezer unashamedly revealed the deeper motivations and springs of his life. This is witnessed to by Robert St. John in his biography of this giant Zionist:

> He locked himself in his study and spent his time working on the dictionary and the manuscript for the Hebrew classics. Occasionally he wrote an editorial for his son's newspaper, which now, in the date line, gave the year in two ways: so many years after the destruction of the Temple, and so many years after the issuance of the Balfour Declaration. ... The prayer shawl which Ben Yehuda had worn in his early days in Jerusalem, when he was trying to win the support of the Orthodox group, he now wore for no other reason than that he wished to.
>
> His new attitude toward his old religion perplexed many people. There were some who thought it was a pose, a new trick. There were some who questioned his sincerity.
>
> But one of Ben Yehuda's friends one day silenced a particularly vocal doubter by saying:
>
> "I was in the Hurva Synagogue the day the end of the Third Exile was officially pronounced. Ben Yehuda was also there. I was near enough to him so I could see the tears streaming down his face. I saw the look in his eyes.
>
> "I knew then what I had always suspected. Down underneath it all Ben Yehuda has a deeply religious soul. He has fought superstition and bigotry and fanaticism, but that does not mean he is not a good and a humble man."

In these last days of his life Eliezer Ben Yehuda began to experience an inner serenity which all those about him observed.(156)

I have quoted in full several of these amazing passages from the history of some of the great Zionist leaders to show from what sorrow and suffering, but also deep faith and prayer, the modern Zionist movement was born. I have especially done so because people from various political and religious backgrounds have—and still do—often malign this beautiful, Bible-based movement as a sinister, man-made, conspiratorial, political movement that could not possibly have been from God. Nothing is further from the truth.

I want to draw this chapter to a close with a prayer Jews pray in synagogues at their three major feasts—the Feast of Passover, the Feast of Weeks and the Feast of Tabernacles. It is a prayer prayed by millions of Jews throughout their years of dispersion:

> By reason of our sins we have been exiled from our land and removed far from our native soil, so that we are no longer able to go up and appear and prostrate ourselves before Thee…because of the violent hand that has been laid upon Thy sanctuary…. Reveal the splendor of Thy majesty and reign over us in the sight of all living. Approximate our scattered ones from amongst the nations, and assemble our dispersed ones from the extremities of the earth. Bring us unto Zion, Thy city, in jubilation, and unto Jerusalem, the place of Thy House, in everlasting joy.

And on the Sabbath they have prayed,

> For in Thy Holy Name, great and sublime, do we confide; we rejoice in Thy salvation. Cause us to return in peace from the four corners of the earth unto our own land, for the God that worketh salvation art Thou…. In Thy inexhaustible benevolence, sustain us and gather our dispersed in Thy holy place, that they may observe Thy commands and serve Thee with a pure heart….

O Lord, our God and God of our fathers, may it be Thy will to rebuild the Temple speedily in our days, that we may serve Thee in accordance with Thy will.... Cause us to rejoice, Lord our God, by the coming of Thy prophet Elijah, and by the restoration of the Kingdom of David, Thy chosen one. May His Kingdom speedily restore the joy in our hearts, and let no stranger sit on the throne of David and no longer tarnish his glory....

In response to all these prayers, and the sufferings and agony of His own people, God responds in a most amazing yet tender way:

"Heaven is My throne, and earth is My footstool. Where is the house that you will build Me ? And where is the place of My rest? For all those things My hand has made, and all those things exist," says the Lord. "But on this one I will look: on him who is poor and of a contrite spirit, and who trembles at My word...Who has heard such a thing? Who has seen such things? Shall the earth be made to give birth in one day? Or shall a nation be born at once? For as soon as Zion was in labor [as soon as Zion travailed], she gave birth to her children. Shall I bring to the time of birth, and not cause delivery?" says the Lord. "Shall I who cause delivery shut up the womb?" says your God. "Rejoice with Jerusalem, and be glad with her, all you who love her; rejoice for joy with her, all you who mourn for her; that you may feed and be satisfied with the consolation of her bosom, that you may drink deeply and be delighted with the abundance of her glory."
Isaiah 66:1–2,8–11 (NKJV, KJV)

After nearly 2,000 long years of waiting, of suffering, of humiliation, of massacre, of untold agony, but also of hope and prayers, it finally happened.

The Jews came home from the four corners of the earth, from the North—from Europe, from the South—from Egypt, Yemen, Morocco, from the West and from the East, back to the land that had waited for them for all these centuries. Finally the day announced by the psalmist had come: *"You will arise and have mercy on Zion; for the time to favor her, yes, the set time, has come."* Psalms 102:13

A nation would be born in a day, and after nearly 2,000 pain-filled years, it finally happened. Israel was born anew on May 14, 1948.

Claude Duvernoy writes,

May 15 was a Saturday, a Sabbath. It was symbolic that this day should be the day of rest, for Israel could at long last rest from its twenty-centuries-long martyrdom, and God was praised in every synagogue. In Rome, Jews sang and wept with joy under the Arc of Titus, which commemorates the defeat of the Jewish armies and the destruction of Jerusalem in the year 70. David Ben-Gurion, the Joshua redivivus, proclaimed in the Declaration of Independence:

"...The State of Israel will open its gates to Jewish immigrants from all the countries of Exile; it will apply itself to the development of the country for the benefit of all its inhabitants; it is founded on the principles of freedom, justice and peace proclaimed by the prophets of Israel.... We put our trust in the Rock of Israel."(157)

Chapter Eleven

Why Israel Is Hated

Yes, the State was born, but the moment she was born—just as with the newly born Christ in Bethlehem—evil forces wanted to attack and strangle Israel. Seven Arab armies—of Egypt, Jordan, Syria, Iraq, Lebanon, Saudi Arabia and the forces of the Mufti of Jerusalem—invaded and attacked her when she had barely finished dancing and rejoicing in the streets of Jerusalem and other cities and towns across the land.

In a way, it has always been like that in Israel's history. In Psalms 83 we find these words:

O God, do not remain quiet; Do not be silent and, O God, do not be still. For behold, Your enemies make an uproar, And those who hate You have exalted themselves. They make shrewd plans against Your people, And conspire together against Your treasured ones. Psalms 83:1–3 (NAS)

Satan has always hated Israel. Before the Exodus from Egypt, he stirred the heart of Pharaoh against them. Before the Exodus from

Media and Persia, he used Haman's jealousy of Mordecai to concoct a plan to murder them all. Later, he had Hitler on his side to prevent the third homecoming of the Jewish people and to massacre them while they were still in Europe. It had always been that way, and now that the Jews were back and finally had their State after two long millennia, his anger was stirred again.

To understand the anger of the Arabs against God's people, the Jews, and their homecoming and subsequently reborn State, we need to look at the origins of this hatred.

There is an excellently researched book about this written by Joan Peters. *From Time Immemorial* (158) is widely accepted as the definitive work on the subject. It is probably one of the books that the enemies of Israel hate and fear the most. I will quote extensively from it.

Just as there was a definite ideology behind the hatred and atrocities of Hitler and the Nazis, there is one behind the hatred and wars by the Arabs against the Jews and people of Israel. It is not just a question of "their land" being taken; it has far deeper origins, one of the principle ones being the influence and ideology of Islam.

No one who disregards or fails to study the Islamic aspect of the conflict will ever understand the real reasons for the bitter hatred and ongoing battle against little Israel. Let me, therefore, begin with some excerpts from the recently published *Covenant of the Islamic Resistance Movement* (Hamas).

> The Islamic Resistance Movement is one of the links in the chain of the struggle against the Zionist invaders...it goes on to reach out and become one with another chain, that includes the struggle of the Palestinians and Moslem brotherhood.... The Islamic Resistance Movement aspires to the realization of Allah's promise, no matter how long that should take. The Prophet, Allah bless him and grant him salvation, has said: "The Day of Judgment will not come about until Moslems fight the Jews" (killing them).

The Islamic Resistance Movement believes that the land of Palestine is an Islamic Waqf consecrated for future Moslem generations until Judgment Day.

There is no solution for the Palestinian question except through Jihad. Initiatives, proposals and international conferences are all a waste of time and vain endeavors.

Article 14: The question of the liberation of Palestine is bound to three circles:

> The Palestinian circle,
> The Arab circle and
> The Islamic circle.

Each of these circles has its role in the struggle against Zionism.(159)

This last point is critical if one is to understand the major factors inherent in the Middle East conflict. All three circles are Muslim. Although in one way they are separate, they work under that unifying influence of Islam, together aiming for the universally declared Muslim goal—that Palestine as a country will revert to Islamic rule and sovereignty. That, in short, is the crux of the whole Middle East conflict. To see whether this really is the case, we shall document it in numerous ways.

Today, most of the relatively uninformed journalists and politicians in the West are of the misguided opinion that as long as Israel withdraws from the "occupied territories," namely, Gaza, Judea and Samaria (the "West Bank") and the Golan Heights, there will be a chance for peace in the Middle East.

The reason they think this is their false perception of the conflict as being basically over land—rather than the reality that what is being sought is the elimination of Israel from the map of the Middle East. This can easily be understood simply by taking a closer look at the history of the region.

During the Six Day War, Egyptian President Gamal Abdel Nasser was not commanding his army and soldiers to liberate Gaza and the

"West Bank"—these lands were already in Arab hands, in Egypt's and Jordan's hands!

No, Nasser was telling his troops to slaughter the Jews, to destroy Israel. The battle was not for the "West Bank," but for the destruction of the State of Israel in the name of Allah and Islam.

After all, the PLO was formed in 1964, three years *before* the "West Bank" was brought under Israeli sovereignty in the Six Day War of self-defense. What this means is that rather than to liberate the "West Bank"—which was already in Arab hands—the PLO was formed to "liberate" *all* of Palestine from Jewish sovereignty, as its name signifies.

If it had been a simple question of dividing up the land between two peoples—the Jews and the Arab Palestinians—then the Arabs had ample opportunity during 1947, when the United Nations resolution suggested just that—the partition of the land into states for the Arabs and the Jews. The Arabs—not the Jews—refused to accept this partition plan because they wanted it all: Tel Aviv—Jaffa—Haifa—all of it!

But the Middle East conflict is "sold" by the Muslims and the Arabs to a gullible world as the Jews' theft of Arab lands. The opposite is true: the Arabs declared war on Israel in 1948 because they (the Arabs) wanted to also have the land which the United Nations had set aside (partitioned) for the Jews. *That* is why there has been war in the Middle East for almost 50 years.

There is another thing to be noted. The original land of the Palestine Mandate, set aside by the League of Nations and the Balfour Declaration for the Jews to establish their homeland, included the land both east and west of the Jordan River, which made up both eastern and western Palestine.

However, even though the whole land—both eastern and western Palestine—had been meant for Jewish settlement and as a Jewish homeland, the British, under Arab pressure, unilaterally carved out 75 percent of the area to placate the Hashemite, King Faisal. Thus,

> ...the "native soil" of Arab and Jewish "Palestines" each gained independence within the same two-year period. Transjordan in 1946 (given to Abdullah) and Israel in 1948."(160)

And yet even this was not enough for the Arabs. Israel had to be completely destroyed. Forget about the fact that the joint territory occupied by the descendents of Ishmael is 614 times larger than what was left to Israel—614 times! That is twice the size of the United States. Still the Arabs and the Muslims were not content—any piece of Palestine in the hands of the Jewish infidels was an unbearable affront to Allah—it, all of it, had to be brought back into the Muslim fold. The Arab states have backed the PLO as the instrument with which to realize their goal.

The PLO Covenant, which virtually bespeaks this same aim—the destruction of the State of Israel—in the end enjoys the backing of all the Arab Muslim states which have, by unanimous decision, made the PLO the sole legitimate representative of the Palestinian people. Not one of these Arab states is on record as having ever requested the official removal or modification of those articles in the PLO's charter which call point-blank for the destruction of the sovereign State of Israel. Why not? Because, in fact, none of the Arab nations, when they get down to it, really object to these paragraphs.

As the aforementioned *Covenant of the Islamic Resistance Movement* says, there are three movements, or circles, all cooperating to reach the same goal—the elimination of Israel. The Palestinian circle, the Arab circle and the Muslim circle have basically no dispute about their final aim—the uprooting from their Islamic midst of the cancerous growth—Israel.

That is why the PLO gave so much support to and cooperated with the Ayatollah Khomeini. Though he was not an Arab, he could be trusted as a fanatical Muslim to be part of the struggle against the Jews. Khomeini received a lot of help from Arafat, who, when he kissed and embraced the ayatollah after the successful revolution, said, "This embrace is for the liberation of Jerusalem and Palestine!"

Let us clearly remember that none of the Arab nations, nor the further-off Islamic states, have ever demanded that Arafat or the PLO change the organization's charter. Why? Again, because the underlying yearning for the destruction of the Jewish state still lives in the hearts of millions of Muslims—be they Arab, Iranian, Indian or Malaysian Muslims, it makes no difference. Ask them and they will tell you: it is the will of Allah that Israel be destroyed.

This was what one of the very first Muslim Palestinian Arab leaders, the Grand Mufti of Jerusalem, Haj Amin al Husseini, stated when he was hosted, together with Hitler, on Berlin Radio in 1942: "Kill the Jews—kill them with your hands, kill them with your teeth— this is well pleasing to Allah."

Curiously, Arafat was a blood relative of Haj Amin al Husseini, as is Faisal Husseini, one of today's main spokesmen for the Palestinian delegation to the "Middle East Peace Talks."

Arafat was born in 1929 and died in 2004. His full name, as registered by his father Abdul in Cairo's interior ministry, was Rahman Abdul Rauf Arafat Al-Qudwa Al-Husseini. Arafat was the name of a sacred mountain near Mecca where Muhammad, according to Islamic belief, was transformed into the final messenger of Allah.

In his early years, Arafat came under the strong influence and teaching of the Muslim teacher, Yusuf al-Akbar, with whom he spent many hours. By the time Rahman was eight, he was spending more time in al-Akbar's company than with his family. Al-Akbar brainwashed Arafat, convincing him that he had a special role to play. Thus the Islamic effect on the young Arafat was the first and strongest influence in his life. This explains why the former PLO chief was always able to relate well to the most fanatical Muslim leaders, even if there were periods of estrangement and rivalry, as in his relationship with Libyan leader, Muammar Qaddafi.

So once again we are confronted with the predominant influence of Islam on today's Palestinian Arab struggle against Israel. What were the origins of Islam? Why has it caused such destruction wherever it has spread?

It was in the Night of Power—as it is termed—in the Month of Abstinence, that Muslims believe the angel Gabriel first appeared to Mohammed. Macbride says in *"Mohammedan Religion Explained,"*

> After this appearance…there is said to have been an intermission of two years, during which [Mohammed] suffered hallucination of his senses, and several times contemplated self-destruction. His friends were alarmed, and called in exorcists, and he himself doubted the soundness of his mind. Once he said to his wife, "I hear a sound and see a light: I am afraid there are gins (spirits) in me;" and again, "I am afraid I am a Kahin," that is, a soothsayer possessed by Satan. "God", replied Khadijah, "will never permit this, for thou keepest thy engagements, and assistest thy relatives;" and, according to some, she added, "Thou wilt be the prophet of thy Nation." These sounds, as from a clock or a bell, are enumerated as symptoms of epilepsy. In this morbid state of feeling he is said to have heard a voice, and on raising his head, beheld Gabriel, who assured him he was the prophet of God. Frightened, he returned home, and called for covering. He had a fit, and they poured cold water on him; and when he came to himself he heard those words, "Oh, thou covered one, arise, and preach, and magnify thy Lord;" and henceforth, we are told, he received revelations without intermission. Before this supposed revelation he had been medically treated on account of the evil eye; and when the Koran first descended to him he fell into fainting fits, when, after violent shudderings, his eyes closed, and his mouth foamed. Khadijah offered to bring him to one who would dispossess him of the evil spirit, but he forbade her.(161)

If this fails to indicate the strange origins of Islam, then perhaps we should look at the fruits and consequences that accompanied the spread of the religion. Wherever Islam went it subdued people by the sword and perpetrated horrible massacres, all in the name of Allah.

This has been well documented by Bat Ye'or in her two books, *The Dhimmi: Jews and Christians Under Islam*(162) and, in French, *Les Chrétienté d'Orient Entre Jihad et Dhimmitude,*(163) which chronicle the unbelievable destruction of Christian communities all over the Middle East as a result of the spread of Islam.

As the Muslims grew increasingly powerful, the Holy War spread out beyond Arabia. Initially a razzia for spoils, the *jihad* developed into a war of conquest subject to a code of legislation, the principal aim of which was the conversion of the infidels. Truces were allowed but never a lasting peace. Polytheists generally had to choose between death or conversion; life, freedom of worship, and the inviolability of their belongings was, on certain conditions, conceded to Jews, Christians, and Zoroastrians, and later, of necessity, to Hindus.

The *jihad* is a global conception that divides the peoples of the world into two irreconcilable camps: that of the *dar al-Harb,* the "Territory of War," which covers those regions controlled by the infidels; and the *dar al-Islam,* the "Territory of Islam," the Muslim homeland where Islamic law reigns. The *jihad* is the normal and permanent state of war between the Muslims and the *dar al-Harb,* a war that can only end with the final domination over unbelievers and the absolute supremacy of Islam throughout the world. In the fourteenth century, a jurist, Ibn Taymiyya, justified this permanent state of war by asserting that because the possession of lands by infidels is illegitimate, such lands should revert by Divine Right to the adherents of the true religion. Thus the *jihad* became the means by which the Muslims *received back* that which had been usurped on earth by the infidels. In this sense it is a holy and legitimate war because it *restored* to the Muslims the lands and possessions that should be a part of the *dar al-Islam*, but which the *dar al-Harb* retains illegally. For that reason, any warlike act in the *dar al-Harb*—which has no legal right to exist—may be regarded as just and legitimate and is exempt from any moral disapproval....

Muslim jurists fixed the rights of conquest on the basis of Muhammad's treatment of the Jews of Arabia. This treatment became a model serving as a universal norm to be applied to all Jews, Christians, Zoroastrians, and others vanquished by *jihad.* In the same manner as Muhammad had spared the Jews of Khaybar, who had recognized his suzerainty (sovereignty), so the Arab conquerors concluded "toleration" treaties with all the other peoples who, faced with *jihad,* submitted to their domination. The *dhimmi* condition, which is a direct consequence *of jihad,* is connected with this same contract. It suspends the conqueror's initial rights over the adherents of the revealed religions on payment of a tribute such as the Jews had agreed to give the Prophet at Khaybar.(164)

The term "Islamization" refers to a complex political, economic, cultural, religious and ethnical process by which the Islamized populations of Arab or Turkish background took over the people, civilizations and local religions of the countries they invaded. In this process one can notice two different factors: fusion—the absorption of local civilizations by the invaders, conversions of the people of the land to Islam; and conflicts—massacres, slavery, deportations and systematic destruction of the local civilizations in their cultural and religious forms or expression. This evolution does not rule out the simultaneous coexistence of conflictual and fusion situations. This process has been used in countries such as Armenia, Persia, Syria, Palestine, Egypt, North Africa, Cyprus, Crete, Spain, France and Italy.(165)

Joan Peters writes,

...the Prophet Muhammad's original plan had been to induce the Jews to adopt Islam; when Muhammad began his rule at Medina in A.D. 622 he counted few supporters so he adopted several Jewish practices—including daily prayer facing toward Jerusalem and the fast of Yom Kippur—in the hope of wooing the Jews. But the Jewish community rejected the Prophet Muhammad's religion, preferring to adhere to its own beliefs, whereupon Muhammad subsequently substituted Mecca for Jerusalem, and dropped many of the Jewish practices.

Three years later, Arab hostility against the Jews commenced, when the Meccan army exterminated the Jewish tribe of Quraiza. As a result of the Prophet Muhammad's resentment, the Holy Koran itself contains many of his hostile denunciations of Jews and bitter attacks upon the Jewish tradition, which undoubtedly have colored the beliefs of religious Muslims down to the present.(166)

In 1970, Yasser Arafat stated,

The liberation of Palestine, and putting an end to Zionist penetration—political, economic, military and propaganda—into Moslem States, is one of the duties of the Moslem world. We must fight a holy war *(jihad)* against the Zionist enemy, who covets not only Palestine but the whole Arab region.(167)

For those who fail to see the relevance of the Bible to Zionism and Israel, it may be interesting to know that at least Israel's enemies take it seriously:

In July 1982 UNESCO passed a resolution demanding that the history related by the [Jewish] Bible be rewritten so that the Jews were left out of it.(168)

This came after a visit in October 1980 when Yasser Arafat had addressed the UNESCO conference in Belgrade with a blistering attack on Zionism.

Even as recently as 1981 the Muslim countries—gathered together for their third Islamic Summit conference at Taib, Saudi Arabia—obliged Arafat's wish when they stated in the fifth resolution,

> The Islamic countries made it clear in their resolution that the word *jihad* is used in its Islamic sense, which is not susceptible to interpretation or misunderstanding, and that the practical measures for its implementation will be taken in conformity with this and in constant consultation between the Islamic countries.(169)

Thus, we see from all the above, that the Islamic factor in the Middle East conflict, although overlooked by most politicians, has been one of the most powerful and dangerous of all. This is what Israel's President Herzog tried to impress upon the Europeans when addressing parliamentarians in Strasbourg in 1992:

> It is the rise of Islamic fundamentalism which threatens the regimes of most of the Middle East today, which sponsors uprisings…in many countries in our region and which is spreading rapidly throughout the world.

Homing in on the growing concern over attempts by Islamic states to acquire nuclear, chemical and biological weaponry, President Herzog warned that when the extremism of Islamic fundamentalism was linked to the terror of weapons of mass destruction, "one cannot escape a formula for catastrophe."

In his book on Islam, my Palestinian Arab friend, Dr. Anis Shorrosh, wrote the following:

> At the Battle of Tours, France, in AD 732, the Muslims were stopped in their tracks as their armies advanced to

conquer the world. But now the cry is intensifying, as we heard in England in the summer of 1985: "If we can take London for Islam, we can take the world." Their effort is militant, represented by men like Ayatollah Khomeini of Iran, military regimes like Colonel Qaddafi of Libya and the tragic civil war in Lebanon.(170)

The British high commissioner and commander in chief in Palestine, J.R. Chancellor wrote on September 1, 1929,

> I have learned with horror of the atrocious acts committed by bodies of ruthless and blood-thirsty evildoers, of savage murders perpetrated upon defenceless members of the Jewish population, regardless of age and sex—acts of unspeakable savagery.(171)

Joan Peters writes,

> The violence that the PLO's Yasser Arafat and others now claim was "only begun against Jews with the 1948 rebirth of Israel"—"Palestinian" terrorism—was actually a critical factor in the early developments that instigated the pivotal population conditions in Palestine. In their Holy Land, the Jews, as well as Christians, suffered long from harsh discrimination, persecution, and pogroms. According to the British Consulate report in 1839, the Jew's life was not "much above" that of a dog.(172)

That this was not just the case for Jews and Christians in the Holy Land, but also for those living as they did as *dhimmies* under Muslim rule for centuries in other parts of the Middle East, is amply documented in Bat Ye'or's "The Dhimrni."

In *The Closed Circle,* David Pryce-Jones writes,

> On November 28, 1941, [the Mufti of Jerusalem] Haj Amin met Hitler. They were in accord about the necessity of *destroying Jews everywhere* (Ed. note: Not just in Israel as the Palestinian Arabs would like the gullible world to

believe!), but Hitler refrained from committing himself to the liberation of the Arabs.... Making himself a useful ally, Haj Amin became a war criminal. A German-Arab training detachment had already been recruited among Arab volunteers in Germany, wearing the German uniform with an armband *"Frei Arabien."* Haj Amin's military commander, Qawukji had also reached Berlin, and with his help the training detachment was enlarged into an Arab legion. The legion was open to other Muslims, for instance Bosnians, and in the end it became an SS unit. Haj Amin early appreciated the importance of Himmler and placed himself under his particular sponsorship, prompting him in a series of letters and appeals—superfluous, to be sure—to block escape routes for Jews in the Balkans and elsewhere, and to pursue their exterminations.... Haj Amin was declaring, "Kill the Jews wherever you find them—this pleases God, history and religion." He played his part fully in aiding and abetting mass murder. Hitler came to believe that greater use might have been made of the Arabs, saying in February 1945 with regret that the Arabs might have served as "our best card" because "the Islamic world was quivering in the expectation of our victory."(173)

Enough has been said to show that the underlying reason for the hatred against the Jews and Israel has little to do with finding a just solution for the Palestinian Arabs—the story successfully sold to the world. The "just solution" that was pursued by the Palestinian Arabs under the leadership of the PLO—backed first and foremost by all other Muslim Arab nations and then by the whole Muslim world at large—was the destruction and obliteration of Israel. There was an obvious similarity between the slogans of the Nazis and the Muslim Arabs, the Nazis wanting to purge the Aryan race of Jewish "vermin," and the Muslim Arabs wanting to purge the blood of Islam of the Jewish state and sovereignty—the "cancer."

It certainly makes sad reading, especially for the Jewish people who long so desperately to live in peace with their neighbors.

Let us not forget, with all the talk about the Palestinian Arab refugees who fled from Israel during the War of Independence in 1948, that an equal number of Jews fled from Arab countries and that these Jewish refugees left far more land, bank accounts, houses, furniture and other belongings in Arab hands than the Palestinian Arabs who fled from Israel left behind. Therefore, in the *de facto* population exchange that took place, the Arabs were the winners—they received and pocketed far more wealth and property from the Jews who had fled from their countries, than everything which the Arabs who fled Israel had left behind them.

Terrence Prittie, former editor of the *Manchester Guardian,* has written a booklet about this amazing phenomenon which he called *The Double Exodus.* In it he writes,

> The Arabs of Haifa followed the instructions of their own National Committee, and left. Even the woman hijacker, Leila Khaled, who claimed that she had been "driven" from her home, admitted that she was in fact driven away in a taxi—ordered by her mother in direct disregard of the absent father's instructions to the family to stay where they were.

> The attempt of the Jewish authorities to stop the Arabs fleeing was noted in a report on April 28 by the British Superintendent of Police in Haifa:

> "There is no change in the situation in Haifa. The Jews are still making every effort to persuade the Arab populace to remain and settle back into their normal lives in the town."

> Jewish efforts to stem the flow of refugees was also noted by British journalists on the spot—as in this account by a special correspondent of the *Economist:*

"During subsequent days the Jewish authorities, who were now in complete control of Haifa (save for limited districts still held by the British troops) urged all Arabs to remain in Haifa and guaranteed them protection and security. As far as I know, most of the British civilian residents whose advice was asked by Arab friends told the latter that they would be wise to stay. However, of the 62,000 Arabs who formerly lived in Haifa, not more than 5,000 or 6,000 remained. Various factors influenced their decision to seek safety in flight. There is but little doubt that the most potent of these factors were the announcements made over the air by the Arab Higher Executive, urging all Arabs in Haifa to quit. The reason given was that upon the final withdrawal of the British, the combined armies of the Arab States would invade Palestine and drive the Jews into the sea, and it was clearly intimated that those Arabs who remained in Haifa and accepted Jewish protection would be regarded as renegades".... Statements have been made on the Arab refugee question, but why should the State of Israel be blamed for the existence of that problem? When seeking to determine responsibility for the existence of the problem of the Arab refugees, we cannot fail to mention the outside forces.... They pursue their own selfish interests...which have nothing in common either with the cause of peace and international security or with the interests of the Arab and Jewish peoples, and which only correspond to the aggressive designs of the leading circles of some states.(174)

Following are excerpts from an article in Arabic by Sabri Jrayyis, a well-known Palestinian Arab researcher at the Institute for Palestinian Studies in Beirut, published in *Al-Nahar*, Beirut, May 15, 1975:

"It is not true that foreign States, especially Czarist Russia, Nazi Germany, Britain and the United States, were the only agents behind the conditions that led to the creation of Israel. The Arabs also took part in the process; sad to say, they were very active in it. When Israel was established, on 14 May 1948, it had an estimated population of 650,000 Jews. Today the number is three million, of which half-a-million came to Israel during the last twenty-seven years from eight Arab states, all currently members of the Arab League and representing every type of regime that exists in the Arab world: monarchic, revolutionary, socialist and progressive. This is hardly the place to describe how the Jews of the Arab states were driven out of the countries in which they lived for hundreds of years, then how they were shamefully deported to Israel after their property had been confiscated or taken over at the lowest possible price....

It is plain that Israel will air this issue in the course of any serious negotiations that might be undertaken one day in regard to the rights of the Palestinians....

Israel's claims are these: It may perhaps be the case that we Israelis were the cause of the expulsion of some Palestinians, whose number is estimated at 700,000, from their homes during the 1948 War, and afterwards took over their properties. Against this, since 1948, you Arabs have caused the expulsion of just as many Jews from the Arab States, most of whom settled in Israel after their properties had been taken over in one way or another. Actually, therefore, what happened was only a kind of 'population and property exchange,' and each party must bear the consequences. Israel is absorbing the Jews of the Arab States; the Arab States, for their part, must settle the Palestinians in their own midst and solve their problems.

There is no doubt that, at the first serious discussion of the Palestinian problem in an international forum, Israel will put these claims forward."(175)

There is, therefore, no reason not to believe God's view of things. The Arab nations (although, of course, not the individual Arabs who have been left to suffer by their own leaders) have been amply paid back for all the Arab property abandoned in Israel when they fled—by all the property that came their way from the Jews who fled from their midst.

We have seen some of these deep-rooted causes of the present battle against Israel—a battle we should expect if the restoration of Israel is directly linked to the redemption of this planet Earth, as the Bible says. If this is the case, then we can expect, as has always happened in the history of Israel, that enormous powers and influences will be brought against her. This truly has happened and continues to happen. The evil one will not give up his fight against God's purposes so easily, especially as they concern the apple of His eye— His people Israel.

Chapter Twelve

The Battle for the Land

When, under Joshua, Israel finally came into the land of promise after 40 years of wandering in the wilderness, what awaited them was certainly no picnic.

For a long time there were difficult and painful battles with the different people in the land and later with the surrounding countries—Syria, Ammon, Moab, Egypt, and others. Therefore, it should not surprise us that everything has not gone smoothly during the current return to their land. There has been, and there will continue to be, a lot of resistance to God's plan with Israel. We need to keep cool heads and not become so "spiritually minded" that we lose sight of the modern-day realities Israel faces.

On the whole, we can say that under the extreme circumstances menacing Israel from the date of her rebirth (and before) to the present day, she has—with possibly some exceptions—fared better than most of the world's nations would have under similar circumstances.

As of now, and following the terrible Holocaust experience in which six million of her people died, Israel has fought five wars:

- The War of Independence(1948)
- The Sinai Campaign(1956)
- The Six Day War(1967)
- The Yom Kippur War(1973)
- The Peace for Galilee War(1982)

Besides these, Israel has suffered numerous casualties through acts of terror—perpetrated both in Israel and all over the world against her citizens—and during the long and painful years of the *intifada.*

On top of this, Israel was attacked 39 times during the Persian Gulf War, when Saddam Hussein showered her with Scud missiles. During these attacks, as they watched the rockets descending upon the Israeli population centers, Palestinian Arabs in the state were dancing on their roofs shouting *"Allahu Akbar"* (Allah is great).

What is truly remarkable is that, after all this Arab-perpetrated suffering, war and violence, Israelis still have so much understanding for the Palestinians and show a willingness to live together with them as much as they will allow.

The peace process—begun under the *Likud*-led government of Prime Minister Yitzhak Shamir, first in Madrid and later in Washington, DC—is proof of this tremendous desire by any Israeli administration to reach a just and lasting *modus vivendi* with those who, to date, have invested most of their time in conspiring against the well-being of Israel. They have tried every means to defeat her: through war, through terrorism, through hate propaganda, through trade boycott, by burning Israel's carefully planted and nurtured forests, by stoning and stabbing innocent Israelis, by blowing up civilian aircraft, by killing their Olympic athletes, by filling Israel's oranges with mercury, by burning their cars, by killing or wounding their diplomats, by threatening their friends, by bombing their synagogues or other public places. Nothing and nobody has been safe, and yet Israel, with inexhaustible and admirable patience, has continued trying to come to peace with those whose own covenant declares that their aim is the complete dismantling of the State of Israel. How astounding! And how much more amazing that most of the nations of the world still criticize Israel instead of the Arabs who, as former Israeli ambassador to the United Nations, Abba Eban, put it, have never missed an opportunity to miss an opportunity to come to a peaceful settlement.

What an amazing world we live in! Jesus said, "... *Jerusalem shall be trodden down of the Gentiles, until the times of the Gentiles be fulfilled.*" Luke 21:24 (KJV). We have seen what spiritual and political currents and influences the Lord has used to have His people return and again become a national state on at least half of their ancient land.

The Jews accepted the partition plan of the United Nations, even though it gave them a far smaller piece of homeland—a mere 16 percent of what was originally demarcated by the Balfour Declaration.

The Arabs objected to even that small sliver of land being partitioned off for the Jewish people and ferociously attacked the newborn state. Thus the Arab-Israeli wars began. The Israelis, though outnumbered and heavily outgunned in 1948, won their War of Independence. The Arabs accepted a ceasefire under the auspices of the United Nations.

Then came the 1956 Sinai campaign, during which the French and the British fought Egypt too. Israel moved right up to the Suez Canal, capturing all the Sinai. Israel's decision to strike against Egypt followed years of Cairo-sanctioned and supported Arab terror raids, launched from Gaza (then illegally occupied by Egypt) against the Jewish state. Between 1949 and 1956, through shellings, military assaults and *Fedayeen* hit-and-run tactics, 1,300 Israelis were killed—four-fifths of them civilian, among them many women and children.

Under tremendous pressure from the United States, and with her French and British allies ending their support, Israel withdrew from the Canal and vacated the Sinai, without obtaining so much as a peace treaty from Egypt in exchange.

On the contrary, Egypt under Gamal Abdel Nasser, filled Sinai with troops, bunkers, fortifications and armaments, thus preparing the large peninsula as a launching pad for the next war against Israel.

In May 1967—barely ten years after Israel, under the full weight of American pressure, withdrew from Sinai and Gaza after her victorious war—Nasser ordered the United Nations Emergency (peace keeping) Forces out of Sinai. Instead of resisting this unilateral Egyptian decision, then UN Secretary General U Thant, willingly complied with Nasser's request and withdrew UNEF. Nasser went on to shout over the airwaves for everyone to hear that this was the hour for which Egypt, the Palestinian Arabs and other Muslim Arabs had waited—the hour when they would drive little Israel into the sea and bring the land of Palestine back under Arab rule.

At the same time, the Egyptian president occupied an island in the Straits of Tiran near Sharm el-Sheikh, thus blocking Israel's southern sea route. This move was recognized internationally as a *casus belli*—an act of war.

Israel's soft-spoken foreign minister, Abba Eban, appealed to the nations of the world to apply diplomatic pressure to Nasser, to urge him to reopen the strait and thereby avert war. Apparently none of the nations held much sway over Nasser, and so Israel was left to sort out her problems herself.

She did so in the early morning hours on Monday, June 5, 1967, when Israeli planes carried out coordinated attacks, swooping down on 11 Egyptian airfields and, in just 170 minutes, smashing 300 of Nasser's 340 fighter planes on the ground and destroying all of his best-equipped air bases. Only 20 Arab planes managed to get into the air, and they, too, were destroyed. This incredible victory sealed the outcome of the war for Israel's defense forces. Without adequate air cover, the Egyptians were no match for the Israeli armored corps.

Nasser, by hardening his heart against the diplomatic pressures put upon him by the Western nations, without realizing it, became himself an instrument of prophecy fulfillment.

God wanted to give His people that part of the land which they did not receive in 1948, and by hardening the hearts of the different Arab leaders—Presidents Nasser and Assad and King Hussein—He impelled Israel to react. The result of what became known as the Six Day War was that Judea and Samaria—heartland of biblical Israel—and the ancient city of Jerusalem—King David's capital—were returned to their original owner.

Even Jordan, whose king had embraced Nasser just before the outbreak of hostilities and had put his army under the control of the Egyptian high command, had been offered a gracious way out by Israeli prime minister Levi Eshkol. General Bull of the United Nations brought King Hussein a letter from Levi Eshkol, telling the king that if he would stop shelling West Jerusalem, Israel would not attack him. King Hussein, having promised his allegiance to Nasser, sent General Bull back with the message that the Israelis could expect him to talk to them only on the battlefield.

Thus, the Lord, by hardening the hearts of the Arab leaders, caused His people Israel to inherit the rest of the land, and especially their ancient city, in a war of self-defense!

Until then, since 1949, Jordan had illegally held and occupied the "West Bank" and Jerusalem. Thus, when Israel recaptured Judea, Samaria and Jerusalem, they did not even take over a territory that legally belonged at that time to any nation! How few in the West have even realized this.

God has His own sovereign way to fulfill His Word and promise.

So, with Judea and Samaria, Jerusalem came back to her original owner, and Israel decided that Jerusalem would never be a divided city again. In 1980, the Israeli Parliament made that decision into a law—Jerusalem would remain "the eternal undivided capital of the State of Israel"!

As a reaction to that law, the Muslim and Arab nations put enormous pressure on those nations which still had their official embassies in Israel's declared capital. Practically all of them withdrew.

It was at this point that the International Christian Embassy Jerusalem was formed in a direct response to the world's cowardice, and especially the cowardice of those nations which, unable to stand up to Arab blackmail, moved their embassies to Tel Aviv.

The International Christian Embassy was birthed on September 30, 1980, during the first public Christian celebration of the Feast of Tabernacles. That celebration brought about 1,000 Christians from different nations and churches to Jerusalem in a show of solidarity with the people of Israel.

Finally, after nearly 2,000 long years, the Jewish people were reunited with their ancient city and capital. Jerusalem—literally trodden under foot by so many different nations—was back in the fold of her own people just as Christ had foretold: ".. *Jerusalem will be trampled by Gentiles until the times of the Gentiles are fulfilled.*" Luke 21:24 The enormous importance of this change of guard has been overlooked, not just by many nations, but by most churches as well. Although it had been foretold by Christ, it failed to ring a bell, even with most of His own followers.

During those days I felt obliged to write an open letter to the American secretary of state, Mr. Alexander Haig, who—although he certainly was not one of Israel's worst critics—had criticized Israel's reunification of Jerusalem. In the letter, which was published in *The Jerusalem Post*, I wrote,

> Sir, The recent statement by the new U.S. Secretary of State concerning the status of Jerusalem, and the implied criticism of the unilateral unification of this city under Israeli sovereignty, came as a disappointment. We did not expect this from the present U.S. administration.
>
> Millions of Christian believers all over the world know that this land was promised to the Jews as an "eternal possession" and that, in due time, after being dispersed, they were to return to this "land of their fathers." This surely included their ancient city of Jerusalem too.

We, therefore, are not opposed to this reuniting of Israel's capital, but oppose the call for internationalization of this city in the name of the interests of the three religions— as if we felt unhappy with the present situation.

Since Israel took control of this city, the rights of the three religious groups—Jews, Christians and Moslems—have been respected. To make a call for a change in the present situation, implying that there is not already this respect granted and guaranteed by Israel, is a deceptive insinuation that is contrary to the truth. In hardly any time in Jerusalem's recent history has such freedom of worship been experienced. Why is this not honestly admitted when nations or religious bodies call for respect of all religious groups in an arrangement of Jerusalem's situation?

Or do the nations suggest that Jordan, which destroyed scores of Jewish synagogues during its administration of the city and illegally barred Jews from entering their own Jewish quarter to pray at the Western Wall, would be a better custodian to guarantee this same respect and freedom for all?

Or would these "concerned people" agree with the resolution of the recent Islamic conference that called for the "West Bank" to become a PLO state with Jerusalem as its capital?

Or would an internationalization of the city be our suggested answer to the city's plight? Does Israel have to believe that in an international arrangement the UN will take better care of this city than Israel is doing now? A UN body that continually manipulates Israel in one-sided criticism, is expected to suddenly become righteous and objective in dealing with Jerusalem? Who will convince the Israelis of such a coming miracle?

Or would Mr. Haig suggest that an international Christian body take control of the affairs of this city, when the institutionalized forms of Christianity are not able to protect their own Christian brethren in Lebanon, neither were they able to guarantee or protect the lives of Jews in Europe from persecution and slaughter? Will they now suddenly prove better custodians of this city than Israel? It must be realized that the Vatican has not yet accepted Israel as a sovereign state, and the World Council of Churches has already forfeited its neutrality by officially condemning Israel's unification of the city without ever making such an official statement during Jordan's illegal and ruinous annexation of the city from 1948 to 1967.

Really, Mr. Haig, what better solution can you suggest for us, than the one we have now under Israel?

The following story, written by an Israeli father, captures something of the intensity and depth of feeling shared among so many Israelis over the reunification of Jerusalem during the Six Day War:

> When the notice arrived, during the 1948 War of Independence, that another of my sons, Yaakov, had been killed in Jerusalem's Old City, I was so badly shocked that for weeks I could not step beyond the threshold of my home. My first son, Moshe Yossef, had previously fallen in the Yron valley.
>
> We did not immediately observe the seven-day mourning period, because Yaakov had not been brought to burial. With a full heart I gathered that day in my home a Minyan (a group of ten), which would enable me to recite the Kaddish Memorial Prayer. Just as I was about to recite it, however, we began taking a terrific shelling, and the men assembled for prayer were forced to scatter.
>
> Thus, I did not recite the first *Kaddish*. For many years I would cast a longing look towards Jerusalem's walls, at

least to gaze in the direction of where Yaakov lay buried. Frequently I would arrange prayer services atop a roof on Mount Zion, just to be able to recite the *Kaddish* as near to the Old City walls as possible.

I knew well that pure souls, such as Yaakov, who died glorifying His Name, were assured of their rightful place alongside the Almighty, and more than he needed the *Kaddish*, I needed it myself in order to extinguish the storm of pain in my heart. It may well be that I also needed it in order to console the Creator of all souls, the Rock of Israel, on the loss to his Chosen People! *Yitgadal ve-yitka-dash*…the godly hymn of memory to the dead and the encouragement of the living.

Thus passed 19 years—years crowned with pride over Israel's rebirth; yet—at the same time—saddened by a Jerusalem rent asunder, and the loss to Israel of the Western Wall and the Tomb of the Forefathers.

Blessed be He who grants good to those who do not deserve it—that we have been privileged to live through the war of 1967—the redemption of Jerusalem and the Western Wall, of Rachel's Tomb, of Hebron and the Burial Cave. Three difficult days passed over our country and its capital. For those who experienced two World Wars and Arab pogroms against the Jews in the past, these three days were difficult ones to bear.

29 Iyar 5727—the day after Jerusalem's liberation— I emerged from nineteen years' imprisonment—to the Old City and the Western Wall. I passed through the Sheikh Jarrakh Quarter, overwhelmed by the intricate fortifications which the Arab Legion had constructed. The heart ached for the hundreds of our boys who had fallen in this war, but I could not help thinking that, if it were not for them and if—God forbid—the enemy had prevailed, what

dimensions the slaughter would have reached. The boys' sacrifice has been atoned.

The streets are littered with rubble and broken glass. Here and there, lies a dead Jordanian soldier. An Arab bus is still burning since yesterday. I reach the Lions' Gate. I kiss Jerusalem's wall, just beyond where stands a small pile of rocks, earth, and rubble, topped by a makeshift sign—in memory of the boys who fell there during the last days.

Almost fearfully, I approach the Western Wall. Rending my shirt, as is the religious custom. I stand before the assembled *Minyan,* leading the afternoon *Minkha* service, and recite the *Kaddish* in memory of my son Yaakov.

After the prayer ends, a dancing circle forms, composed of soldiers and pious *Khassidim.* During the nineteen years, since the passing away of my two sons, I almost never danced. This time, however, I did, with a heaven-piercing song from my throat: "Let the Temple be rebuilt, the City of Zion fulfilled...."

Now it was Shavuot 5727, exactly twenty years later, and I went on a complete tour of the Old City, to honor the ruins of our glorious synagogues, ruined by the hands of Ishmael's sons. And the same question as in the days of biblical Nehemia was posed again: "Shall these stones come alive from among piles of dust? The endurance falters, and the dust is everywhere...."

Later on I turned to where, presumably, my son Yaakov had been buried, alongside tens of others who had fallen for Jerusalem in 1948. It is here, so many years later, that I stood and said *Kaddish* again.

"At the end of days He will send our Messiah.... The Lord, in all His goodness, will bring the dead to life, blessed be His Name for ever and ever."(176)

As we can feel conveyed to us in this moving story of suffering and hope, the return of the Old City during—and as a result of—

the Six Day War was one of the most dramatic events in the young state's history and, according to the Bible, one with world-wide repercussions.

Even if all of the "West Bank," the Golan Heights and the Gaza Strip were to be released to the Arabs for the sake of peace—it would not bring peace. Why? Because no Muslim or Muslim Arab leader would ever agree to the City of Jerusalem remaining in the hands of Jewish infidels. This would be, as they see it, an affront to Allah.

Just as the prophets foresaw that in the end the people of Israel would return to their land, so they also foretold that Jerusalem would become a stumbling block for all the nations. This is already happening in measure today.

Hardly any nation dares to have its embassy in this city—the capital of Israel, indicating that hardly any nation is willing and prepared to really support Israel's right to this unified city as her eternal capital.

The seeds of conflict, just as the Bible predicted, have been planted in this city and, in accordance with the prophets, will again erupt over her.

The nations will reject Israel's claim to Jerusalem and, as a result, will turn against Israel. But God will pour out His indignation on all those nations who dare to come against this city.

> *"And it will come about in that day that I will make Jerusalem a heavy stone for all the peoples; all who lift it will be severely injured. And all the nations of the earth will be gathered against it." Zechariah 12:3 (NAS)*

> *"It shall be in that day that I will seek to destroy all the nations that come against Jerusalem." Zechariah 12:9*

Even as world opinion hardens against Israel, Christians from among the nations will increasingly come to her aid. Both developments are clearly foretold by the prophets. Both are already happening today!

Thus says the Lord of hosts: "Peoples shall yet come, inhabitants of many cities; the inhabitants of one city shall go to another, saying, 'Let us continue to go and pray before the Lord, and seek the Lord of hosts. I myself will go also.' Yes, many peoples and strong nations shall come to seek the Lord of hosts in Jerusalem, and to pray before the Lord." Thus says the Lord of hosts: "In those days ten men from every language of the nations shall grasp the sleeve of a Jewish man, saying, 'Let us go with you, for we have heard that God is with you.'" Zechariah 8:20–23

Thus, Jerusalem will increasingly become a stumbling stone and a dividing issue—she will eventually cause two completely opposite reactions among people: fierce rejection or deep acceptance.

Those who come against her and against Israel will seriously wound themselves as the psalmist already has foreseen:

Let all those who hate Zion be put to shame and turned back. Let them be as the grass on the housetops, which withers before it grows up... Neither let those who pass by them say, "The blessing of the Lord be upon you; we bless you in the name of the Lord!" Psalms 129:5–6,8

But then God will bless those who pray for Jerusalem and who seek her good and the good of the people of Israel.

Pray for the peace of Jerusalem: "May they prosper who love you. Peace be within your walls, prosperity within your palaces." For the sake of my brethren and companions, I will now say, "Peace be within you." Because of the house of the Lord our God I will seek your good. Psalms 122:6–9

This is precisely what we had in our hearts to do when some of us, living as Christians in Israel, saw the nations' shameful rejection of Israel's right to her unified capital. In response to their abandoning Jerusalem, we opened the International Christian Embassy on that sunny day of September 30, 1980, and with about one thousand Christians from different nations and churches, in the presence of the mayor of Jerusalem, we declared,

Dear Mr. Teddy Kollek,

We are here from many different nations of the earth, representing, as we believe, millions of Christians who would have loved to be here with us.

We are thankful that we can be here and say in the name of this multitude, that we are with you at this time. We love you and we pray for your City, in which one day the Messiah will establish His Kingdom of peace and righteousness.

These last weeks must not have been easy for you, as you have seen all the embassies, one after the other, leave Jerusalem where you have worked so hard to create a place where all people could be respected and live in freedom under the same roof of this eternal City.

You have worked hard, very hard, and for the first time in years Jerusalem was an open City where all religions could conduct their affairs in freedom. There was nothing wrong when, in the last UN resolution, it said that Jerusalem should be a city where all religions should practice their faith in freedom. What was wrong, however, was that the UN did not admit that, since the City was united under Israel 13 years ago, this right has already been granted to all! To silence the fact and imply that it is not so, was a gross distortion. But we know better.

Today, we open in this, your City, the International Christian Embassy and, because we believe in God, the God of Israel, and in the promises of His Book, the Bible, we will remain in Jerusalem to pray for its peace and work for its good, knowing that in the end, all shall be well.

May this International Christian Embassy then, be a sign of hope; hope for your people, and hope for your City, so that one day it may become what it was always destined to be under Israel—a new dawn for all mankind.

But why is this city so important—not just for the Jews—but also for everyone in the world who takes the Scriptures seriously?

Jerusalem, in Hebrew, means "the city in possession of peace." In other words, Jerusalem uniquely holds the key to peace in this world, as no other city does. New York can claim to have the United Nations building, Switzerland—Geneva, but in the end it will not be from New York or Geneva that the nations of the world will finally learn to live in peace and justice with one another. It will happen in and from Jerusalem. All the prophets foresaw this day of total glory, peace and righteousness coming to the world and to mankind from this city most despised by the nations—Jerusalem. God will yet lift her up and make her a shining light to the rulers of the world, as the prophet Isaiah so beautifully describes:

> Arise, shine; for your light has come! And the glory of the Lord is risen upon you. For behold, the darkness shall cover the earth, and deep darkness the people; But the Lord will arise over you, and His glory will be seen upon you. The Gentiles shall come to your light, and kings to the brightness of your rising. Lift up your eyes all around, and see: They all gather together, they come to you; your sons shall come from afar, and your daughters shall be nursed at your side... Also the sons of those who afflicted you shall come bowing to you, and all those who despised you shall fall prostrate at the soles of your feet; and they shall call you The City of the Lord, Zion of the Holy One of Israel. Isaiah 60:1–4, 14

The whole chapter of Isaiah 60 is so majestic—so beautiful—so full of the unimaginable future God has in store for His people and their city, that it really should be read in full. Actually, there are many of these futuristic passages in the Bible—passages about the inconceivable future that is coming to the world through the events that will soon come to pass in and around Jerusalem. It is difficult, therefore, to comprehend the absolute blindness or the sheer unwillingness to see among so many of those who call themselves Christians. They still do not see it, even though it is spelled out so very clearly in so many places throughout the Bible!

But here again, it will be either Babylon or Jerusalem to whom people will give their allegiance. One will appear to promise peace and unity, but will conclude in war and destruction. The other will seem to bring division and war, yet will result in a new epoch of peace and righteousness coming to all mankind. One will be based on man's ingenuity and endeavor, the other on God's wisdom and strength. All humankind will have to choose which plan and which city they will uphold.

For the Lord shall build up Zion; He shall appear in His glory. Psalms 102:16

Over the long years of Jewish history, whenever the Jews returned home, it always occurred that God did something remarkable to the world. As Claude Duvernoy remarked,

When they came from Egypt—God descended on Sinai and God made a covenant with His people in fire and thunder.

Then they came back from Babylon and Jesus was born in Bethlehem and the New Covenant was made which included also the Gentiles who would come to faith.

These are the days when, for the third time, the Jewish people have come home, after wandering all over the world for nearly 2,000 years. What will *not* happen this time? The psalmist tells it—"He will appear in glory when He builds up Zion!"

Every time the Jews came home there was so much enemy activity. There was the evil Pharaoh, who was used to try to prevent the first homecoming. There was the jealous, evil-spirited Haman, who nearly exterminated all the Jews before they could come home the second time, from Media and Persia, but whose evil aims were overturned through the prayer and fasting of all the Jews under the leadership of Mordecai and Esther.

And then, in recent times, there was Adolf Hitler and the Nazis, who—again—were used to try to prevent the third and most important homecoming of the Jews. By slaughtering nearly all of those in Europe, the devil this time was nearly successful. And yet God kept a remnant and brought them to their land for the greatest moment in their history.

Therefore, not only has every homecoming of the Jewish people to their promised land resulted in an enormous blessing for mankind, but it also has been preceded every time by a terrific onslaught against the Jewish people to prevent their return home.

On the June 7, 1967, the Old City fell back into the hands of the Jewish people and was reunited with West Jerusalem. Moshe Dayan, coming to the Western Wall, said, "We earnestly stretch out our hands to our Arab brethren in peace, but we have returned to Jerusalem never to part from her again."

Israelis wept and had spiritual experiences at the sight of the Old City, and especially at the sight of the Western Wall.

But had God brought the Jewish people back to end their long history, to stand and pray forever at a piece of wall—however deeply significant that last remaining outer wall of the glorious Temple was?

No thinking person can believe that after nearly 2,000 years of dispersion and untold suffering, persecution, humiliation, massacres, agony and wars, the end result of all this would be Jews standing forever at a part of a wall, to end their quest and journey there. God surely had not brought them back for just this.

So, however crucial and important it is that Jerusalem and the Land of Israel were united again as a result of the Six Day War, there was still no Temple, and Jews were forbidden by the Muslims from going up to the Temple Mount, forbidden even to pray on this Mountain of the Lord where God had dwelt in the Holy of Holies.

The Muslims now claim the Mount exclusively for themselves, forbidding Jews or Christians to pray there. The orthodox Rabbis, out of respect for the place where formerly the Temple and especially the Holy of Holies were located, do not want their people to come up on the Mount in concern that they might inadvertently step on the rectangle where the Holy of Holies once stood.

Yet, there are many Israelis who are praying, hoping and looking to God to bring the glory of His presence back to the Mount, when His house will be built on it again in answer to the many prayers through the centuries in so many synagogues around the world.

One day, during the 1985 celebration of the Feast of Tabernacles, Mayor Teddy Kollek spoke against the background of a painting of Jerusalem which included the sight of the new Temple that the Bible says will one day be rebuilt on the Temple Mount. Welcoming the thousands of Christians who had crammed into the *Binyanei Ha'Uma* auditorium, he said,

> Thank you for being here, for coming here faithfully every year. Your faith gives us strength.... I am glad I am speaking here against the background of this beautiful painting of Jerusalem. It is not yet the Jerusalem of today. If you look properly, you will see that the Temple, the Holy of Holies, has been restored! We believe the Messiah will come; you believe that He will return; He will overcome all difficulties. He will come if we pray. And we all hope it will be soon. Meanwhile, we are grateful for your coming every year expressing this faith of yours and this faith of ours.... Our return is the first sign that the city will be existing again as it is in this painting!

These were the words not of an ultra orthodox Jew or zealous Christian—they were the words of the kind-hearted mayor of Jerusalem, Teddy Kollek, a man known for his sense of justice and fairness toward all religious groupings in this city. Still we, like many Israelis, know that the return to Israel was only the first step—the return in 1967 to Judea and Samaria, to the Western Wall and to the Old City was the second step toward *all* that God has promised to His people by way of the prophets.

Let us listen to the words former Knesset member Geula Cohen wrote after the British withdrawal from Palestine:

> Following the report by the United Nations Special Committee on Palestine, which recommended that the country be partitioned into separate Jewish and Arab states, the British announced that they were planning to evacuate.... Even if the enemy had announced his withdrawal not only from Palestine but from the entire Promised Land, from the borders of the Nile to the banks of the Euphrates, it would not have meant the end of the War of Redemption that we were fighting. Liberating the homeland had never been for us simply a question of ground under our feet, but one of divine imperatives over our lives as well.

> Together with Yair we had taken the oath: "We are soldiers of Israel for life," and we had sworn that there could be no life for Israel without a Kingdom of Israel, the meaning of which was perpetual sacrifice on the fields of holiness and creation. Together with Yair we had sung, "Only death can free us from the ranks"...Somewhere beyond the realms of cold reason, we had believed that, when the last British soldier left the country, messianic times would arrive. Now, however, the British were going home; the veil had fallen, but no Messiah stood behind it.... If the Messiah was not yet in sight, it could only be because the veil hadn't fallen after all.(177)

How deep, therefore, this feeling runs in the hearts of numerous—even so-called secular—Israelis is hidden to many.

One has only to listen to some of the Israeli people to realize what a deep undercurrent this is. We shall surely see some of the most amazing events occur in and around Jerusalem in the coming years. In spite of the evil intent of men and nations in contradiction to that plan of God, He will yet have His way fully and completely. As the psalmist says,

Why do the nations rage,
*   and the people plot a vain thing?*
The kings of the earth set themselves,
*   and the rulers take counsel together, against the Lord*
and against His Anointed, saying,
*   "Let us break Their bonds in pieces and*
cast away Their cords from us."

He who sits in the heavens shall laugh;
*   the Lord shall hold them in derision.*
Then He shall speak to them in His wrath,
*   and distress them in His deep displeasure:*
"Yet I have set My King on My holy hill of Zion."

"I will declare the decree:
*   The Lord has said to Me, 'You are My Son,*
today I have begotten You.
*   Ask of Me, and I will give You*
the nations for Your inheritance,
*   and the ends of the earth for Your possession.*
You shall break them with a rod of iron;
*   You shall dash them in pieces like a potter's vessel.'"*

Now therefore, be wise, O kings;
*   be instructed you judges of the earth.*
Serve the Lord with fear, and rejoice with trembling.
*   Kiss the Son, lest He be angry,*
and you perish in the way,
*   when His wrath is kindled but a little.*
Blessed are all those who
*   put their trust in Him.* Psalms 2:1–12

And as David further prophesies,

For the Lord has chosen Zion; He has desired it for His habitation: "This is My resting place forever; Here I will dwell, for I have desired it. I will abundantly bless her provision; I will satisfy her poor with bread. I will also clothe her priests with salvation, and her saints shall shout aloud for joy. There I will make the horn of David grow; I will prepare a lamp for My Anointed. His enemies I will clothe with shame, but upon Himself His crown shall flourish." Psalms 132:13–18

It is very clear, in the light of these beautiful words, that the redemption of Israel and God's plan with His people certainly will not end at the "Wailing Wall."

Two thousand years of suffering and humiliation, of prayer and hope will not end at the Western Wall. God, as He promised, will restore everything to them, whether the nations like it or not. Of that we can be sure. How He will allow it to happen is up to Him, but we shall surely see amazing events develop in the near future.

He has promised it all through His Word by the prophets of old, and as He has fulfilled the first part, so He will fulfill the rest, so that the nations, however reluctantly, may come to the realization that He is—after all—God! As God says through Ezekiel,

Then they shall dwell in the land that I have given to Jacob My servant, where your fathers dwelt; and they shall dwell there, they, their children, and their children's children, forever; and My servant David shall be their prince forever. Moreover I will make a covenant of peace with them, and it shall be an everlasting covenant with them; I will establish them and multiply them, and I will set My sanctuary in their midst forevermore. My tabernacle also shall be with them; indeed I will be their God, and they shall be My people. The nations also will know that I, the Lord, sanctify Israel, when My sanctuary is in their midst forevermore.
Ezekiel 37:25–28

Chapter Thirteen

The Temple Mount

When the issue of the Temple Mount was being discussed in the United Nations, and the Muslim states strongly condemned any religious use by the Jews of this Temple Mount, we sent the following statement to Israel's ambassador to the United Nations at that time, Mr. Benjamin Netanyahu:

> The International Christian Embassy Jerusalem fervently hopes and prays, that the day will soon come that the Temple Mount—or as the Bible calls it, the Mountain of the Lord—will no longer be a reason for religious divisiveness, but a place where all mankind will unite in worship to God according to His declared purposes.
>
> The Bible foresees the day when all nations will flow to the Mountain of the Lord irrespective of race or color, and says that: "His house shall be called a house of prayer for all nations."

It is against biblical and historical truth for the Muslims to demand that the Temple Mount is their sole property—only allowing the adherents of their faith to pray there.

The Embassy hopes, therefore, that this mountain will not continue to be monopolized exclusively by any group or religion as if it were their sole possession, but that under God it will become the most exalted place to which all mankind can come up, and learn the ways of the Lord, and worship at His footstool, in accordance with the words of the prophet Micah:

Now it shall come to pass in the latter days that the mountain of the Lord's house shall be established on the top of the mountains, and shall be exalted above the hills; and peoples shall flow to it. Many nations shall come and say, "Come, and let us go up to the mountain of the Lord to the house of the God of Jacob; He will teach us His ways, and we shall walk in His paths." For out of Zion the law shall go forth, and the word of the Lord from Jerusalem. He shall judge between many peoples, and rebuke strong nations afar off; they shall beat their swords into plowshares, and their spears into pruning hooks; nation shall not lift up sword against nation, neither shall they learn war any more. Micah 4:1–3

Perhaps the Muslims—who during the earlier part of this century claimed the Wailing Wall as their property, even to the extent of disturbing the Jews when they wanted to pray there, and who now use the Temple Mount to incite Muslims to kill Jews—will one day come to the same conclusion they finally had to accept regarding the Western Wall: It is impossible to kick against the pricks and try to fight against God. At this present time, however, they are as intolerant toward Jews praying on the Jewish Temple Mount as they were in the 1920's toward them praying at their own Wall or *Kotel*.

From 1920 on, during prayer time, a muezzin was deliberately stationed nearby [the *Kotel*] to disturb the

Jewish worshippers with his loud call to prayers. Cattle were driven to and fro in the alleyway leading to the Wall.

This tense situation erupted in 1928 on Yom Kippur when the Arabs removed a cloth paragon that separated— according to Jewish tradition—men and women worshipers during prayers.

The ensuing protest at this act of intolerance ignited the Moslems' fury and resulted in bloody anti-Jewish riots culminating in the massacre of the Jews in Hebron. In 1930, a commission of inquiry was appointed by the British authorities with the approval of the League of Nations. Pleading before the Commission, the Jewish spokesman stated,

"For two-thousand years, this people stood in the open air, in the heat of the sun and the rains of winter, pouring its heart out to God in heaven, and it is denied even this meager right."

The Moslems argued that the Wall was their property and that "Moslems will not surrender to any verdict touching upon their faith even if the entire world approves it."(178)

Thus, Jerusalem is not only important in a general way as the undivided eternal capital of Israel, however important that already is, but there is something much more at stake in the destiny of this city, and that destiny has everything to do with that place which the Lord calls His Holy Hill, where He has desired to dwell among His people forever.

It is this hill—"the Mountain of the Lord"—that is the main reason for the uniqueness and holiness of Jerusalem. As has been said, "It is the most crucial piece of real estate in the whole world."

Jerusalem derives its sanctity much more because of this hill and its future destiny, than from the fact that it is a city sacred to three religions.

No one—literally no one—who is not willing to ponder the ultimate destiny of this hill can fathom the ultimate destiny of Jerusalem.

King David is a wonderful example of at least one man who understood some of the ultimate significance of that hill on which, in his days, the tent or Tabernacle of the Lord stood, enclosing the Ark in the Holy of Holies, and where he used to spend many hours, sometimes also during the night.

David's love for Jerusalem, as expressed in his psalms, stemmed first from his knowledge that it was the city in the midst of which the Lord—whom he had known as a shepherd boy and to whom he sang for so many hours—dwelt. That made the city special for him and, later, for all the house of Israel as they came up to Jerusalem to celebrate their three major feasts. It was not simply because Jerusalem was the capital under King David's and, later, Solomon's reign, but because as they came up to this city they knew Someone lived there whom they worshiped as the God of Israel.

Many of the psalms of David can only be understood in this light. For David, Jerusalem was not just a fantastic, beautiful city and the capital of His Kingdom, nor was it wonderful simply because the Tabernacle (and later the Temple of the Lord) was there.

The most important reason for the uniqueness of Jerusalem was that the Lord was there. It is an amazing thing that the prophet foresaw the day when those words would become the very name of Jerusalem, because they symbolize the very special characteristic of this city: *"...and the name of the city from that day shall be: THE LORD IS THERE."* Ezekiel 48:35

God says through Zechariah,

"I am returning to Jerusalem with mercy; My house shall be built in it," says the Lord of hosts, "and a surveyor's line shall be stretched out over Jerusalem." Zechariah 1:16

... "Jerusalem shall be inhabited as towns without walls, because of the multitude of men and livestock in it."

"For I," says the Lord, *"will be a wall of fire all around her, and I will be the glory in her midst."* Zechariah 2:4–5 (Emphasis added.)

Again,

"Sing and rejoice, O daughter of Zion! For behold, I am coming and I will dwell in your midst," says the Lord... *And the Lord will take possession of Judah as His inheritance in the Holy Land, and will again choose Jerusalem.* Zechariah 2:10,12

Even those who are far away shall come and build the temple of the Lord. Zechariah 6:15

"I am zealous for Zion with great zeal; with great fervor I am zealous for her." Thus says the Lord: "I will return to Zion, and dwell in the midst of Jerusalem. Jerusalem shall be called the City of Truth, the Mountain of the Lord of hosts, the Holy Mountain." Zechariah 8:2–3 (Emphasis added.)

Thus, the uniqueness of Jerusalem certainly does not just lie in its reputation as a city holy to three religions or even just in the fact that it is the capital of Israel. The uniqueness of this city is that it was assuredly God's dwelling place, and although He and His *shekinah* presence left it for a long time, He nonetheless promises, again and again, to come back to Jerusalem in the person of the Son of David, the Messiah King, who will literally rule in this city. He will be the point of attraction, drawing all the rulers and peoples of the world to this city—then risen up as a high mountain—to learn the ways of the Lord.

For the Lord has chosen Zion; He has desired it for His habitation: "This is My resting place forever; here I will dwell, for I have desired it." Psalms 132:13–14

So important is this truth that it is spoken almost identically through two prophets: Micah 4:1-3 (already quoted) and the following passage, Isaiah 2:2-4

Now it shall come to pass in the latter days that the mountain of the Lord's house shall be established on the top of the mountains, and shall be exalted above the hills; and all nations shall flow to it. Many people shall come and say, "Come, and let us go up to the mountain of the Lord, to the house of the God of Jacob; He will teach us His ways, and we shall walk in His paths." For out of Zion shall go forth the law, and the word of the Lord from Jerusalem. He shall judge between the nations, and shall rebuke many people; they shall beat their swords into plowshares, and their spears into pruning hooks; nation shall not lift up sword against nation, neither shall they learn war anymore. Isaiah 2:2–4 (Emphasis added.)

This verse is so clear and magnificent in its description of the wonderful future that still lies ahead for Jerusalem and with its focal point: the soon-coming King and Messiah and the House of the Lord that will be established on the Mountain of the Lord!

All nations shall come up, say the prophets. It will be in the latter day. The result will be world peace and justice. None of these things have ever, as yet, happened in the history of Jerusalem! So either we must conclude that the prophet was fantasizing or that he saw something so great and so all-inclusive that no one can afford to ignore it.

It *is* all-inclusive—praying for Jerusalem's destiny is praying for the redemption of the whole planet, Earth. No wonder it says in Isaiah,

*For Zion's sake I will not hold My peace, and for Jerusalem's sake I will not rest, until her righteousness goes forth as brightness, and her salvation as a lamp that burns. The Gentiles shall see your righteousness, and **all** kings your glory. You shall be called by a new name, which*

the mouth of the Lord will name…J have set watchmen on your walls, O Jerusalem, who shall never hold their peace day or night. You who make mention of the Lord, do not keep silent, and give Him no rest till He establishes and till He makes Jerusalem a praise in the earth. Isaiah 62:1–2,6–7 (Emphasis added.)

Then, and only then, will the earth become a paradise again—a paradise of justice and peace where nations will not fight one another anymore. Nature will be rejuvenated. The Dead Sea will become a sweetwater lake where fish can again swim and glitter in the sunshine of God's light. The trees will clap their hands, and the earth will again be quiet and at rest. The wolf will lie down with the lamb, and the child will play with the serpent. No one will harm anyone, but harmony between nations and people will be restored. Every person will sit in his own garden under his own fig tree. Every year all the nations will come up in joy and happiness to dance and sing in the streets of Jerusalem, during the Feast of Tabernacles. Finally, all that was hoped for and everything that was in the minds of all those who wanted to see a better world come to pass will be realized and will be even better than could be thought or imagined.

Nations, tongues and tribes will come up every year during the glorious reign of the Messiah unto the city of Jerusalem. Not just a colorless mass of mankind—but nations right unto the end, each with its specific color and characteristic. They will come—redeemed—to the Mountain of the Lord—to sing His praises, to participate in that wonderful Feast of Tabernacles each year and be joyful in His presence. It will be a wonderful day—a day of blessing for all mankind as Zechariah so beautifully foresaw:

And it shall come to pass that everyone who is left of all the nations which came against Jerusalem shall go up from year to year to worship the King, the Lord of hosts, and to keep the Feast of Tabernacles. Zechariah 14:16

Therefore, the words spoken by a rabbinical advisor of the Chief Rabbinate of Israel during the international celebration of the Feast of Tabernacles seem highly significant and prophetic:

> Your visit to the Holy City of Jerusalem, the City of David, at this special time of the year is most appropriate.
>
> When the Holy Temple stood in all its glory in Jerusalem 2000 years ago—the sacrificial service during the Festival of Tabernacles commanded a unique universal dimension. Offerings were brought not only for the benefit of the Jewish people but for all the nations of the world...for all mankind.
>
> Regrettably we have no great Temple today, at least not at this moment. But our prayers and worship in synagogues in every corner of the land of Israel are the pending substitutes for those offerings, and at this holy season we pray to God for all humanity.
>
> The wisest of all men, King Solomon, set the tone for the universal nature of the Temple. As the first Temple was completed he offered the following prayer, recorded in First Kings Chapter 8, *"And also the Gentile who is not of your people Israel, when he shall come from afar... and pray in this house, O hear in heaven, the place of Your dwelling and do all that the Gentile shall call upon You...."*
>
> The Prophet Isaiah followed in that same tradition when, in his beautiful and memorable words so fitting to the occasion, he said in Chapter 56:6–7,
>
> *And the Gentile children that join themselves to the Lord to minister unto Him, and to love the name of God, to be his servant... and I shall bring them to my holy mountain, and I shall cause them to rejoice in My house of prayer. Their offerings shall be acceptable on My altar for My house shall be called a house of prayer for all peoples of all nations.*

This very morning in our synagogues, as is customary on every shabbat and festival, we read publicly from the prophets. As it so happened, today's lesson was drawn from the book of Ezekiel, who lived after the sorrowful destruction of the first holy Temple, approximately 2500 years ago. He spoke of that awesome day in the future... When God's name will be magnificent and sanctified and known in the eyes of many nations and they shall know that He is God.

You have come to Jerusalem, the capital of Israel and the spiritual center of the entire world, in recognition of God's special providence with regard to the Jewish people in restoring us to our ancient homeland and strengthening the reborn Jewish State of Israel.

We welcome you with open arms and blessing and thank you for your vital support and efforts on behalf of the Jewish people, Israel and Zionism to realize the prophecy of Isaiah, Chapter 2:

And it shall come to pass in the end of days that the mountain of God's House shall be established at the top of the mountains and shall be exalted above the hills: and all nations shall flow into it. And many peoples shall go and say: Come ye and let us go up to the mountain of the Lord, to the House of the God of Jacob, and He will teach us His ways and we will walk in His paths, for out of Zion shall go forth the Law and the Word of God from Jerusalem. And He shall judge between the nations and shall decide for many peoples and they shall beat their swords into plowshares and their spears into pruning hooks. And nation shall not lift up sword against nation, neither shall they learn war anymore.

Tabernacles—The Feast of Messiah's Appearance

Isn't it significant that it is the Feast of Tabernacles—rather than Passover and Pentecost - that the Bible tells us will be kept during the Messiah's millennial reign, with the added warning that "no rain" will fall on those nations that refuse to attend?

The Christian Zionist Feast of Tabernacles is a feast open to all peoples, as through Zechariah God indicates that the day will come when all nations will be summoned to celebrate the Feast of Tabernacles and worship the King in Jerusalem!

As those of us who have been called out of the nations are witnessing the beginnings of God's restoring of grace and favor to His people, we want to come to Jerusalem now already to rejoice with God and to praise His Name for all He is about to do for Israel. It is therefore the "Feast of the Nations" as the fullness of the Gentiles comes up to Jerusalem. Here we will one day experience with Judah, the Jews, the "Feast of the Double Portions" that will come with the blowing of the Wind of God's Spirit, and the former and the latter rain falling upon God's people in this month!

Thus Tabernacles signifies the restoration of the tabernacle of David, both physically as well as spiritually; the unity of Gentile believers; the fullness of the Gentiles and the people of Israel, and the promised coming blessing of the former and latter rains coming down one day during the Feast.

It is singularly the Feast of Messiah's appearance! **Come and join us this year as we celebrate the LORD God's Feast of Tabernacles!**

For more information on the ICZC Feast of Tabernacles, write to:

International Christian Zionist Center
P.O. Box 49063
Jerusalem 91490, Israel
Email: iczc@iczc.org.il
Website: www.israelmybeloved.com

References

1. Gary H. Kah, *En Route to Global Occupation* (Shreveport, Louisiana: Huntington House Publisher's, 1992), p. 211.
2. Ron Chernow, *The House Of Morgan* (New York: Atlantic Monthly Press, 1990)
3. *The New York Times*, November 16,1987, p. 81.
4. Louis McFadden, *Congressional Record*, 1934, pp. 24,26.
5. William P. Hoar, "Andrew Carnegie," *American Opinion* (Dec. 1975), p. 110, as quoted by A. Ralph Epperson, *The Unseen Hand* (Tucson, Publius Press, 1985), p. 168.
6. Epperson, *Ibid.*, p. 165.
7. Chernow, *op. cit.*, pp. 719–20.
8. Chernow, *Ibid.*, p. 152.
9. Chernow, *Ibid.*, p. 153.
10. Chernow, *Ibid.*, p. 206.
11. Chernow, *Ibid.*, p. 206.
12. Epperson, *op. cit.*, p. 168.
13. Epperson, *Ibid.*, p. 292.
14. Epperson, *Ibid.*, p. 167.
15. Frederick Lewis Allen, *Life Magazine* (April 25,1949).
16. Pat Robertson, *The New World Order* (Dallas: Word Publishing, 1991), p. 66.
17. James Perloff, *The Shadows of Power* (Belmont: Western Islands Publishers, 1988), p. 29.
18. Perloff, *Ibid.*, p. 31.
19. William Greider, *Secrets of the Temple* (New York: Touchstone, 1989), p. 159.
20. Greider, *Ibid.*, p. 135.
21. Perloff, *op. cit.*, p. 72.
22. Gary Allen, "Stop The Bank Gang," *American Opinion* (Feb. 1979), p. 12, as quoted in Perloff, *Ibid.*, p. 73.
23. James Perloff, *op. cit.*, pp. 36–37.
24. Carroll Quigley, *Tragedy and Hope* (New York: Macmillan, 1966), p. 952.
25. Perloff, *op. cit.*, p. 38.
26. Perloff, *Ibid.*, p. 191.
27. Gary Allen, *The Rockefeller File* (California: 76 Press, 1975), p. 61.
28. Perloff, *op. cit.*, cover.
29. Zbigniew Brzezinski, "US Foreign Policy: The Search for Focus," *Foreign Affairs* (July 1973), p. 723.
30. Zbigniew Brzezinski, *Between Two Ages* (New York: Viking Press, 1970), p. 72.
31. Mesarovic, *Mankind at the Turning Point*, p. 203.
32. Jim Lucier, "Bilderbergers," *American Opinion* (Nov. 1964), p. 62.
33. Epperson, *op. cit.*, p. 207.
34. Nesta Webster, *Secret Societies and Subservice Movements* (New York: EP Dutton, 1924), p. 214.
35. Robert W. Lee, *The United Nations Conspiracy* (Belmont: Western Islands Publishers, 1981), p. 98.
36. Lee, *Ibid.*, p. 137.
37. Lee, *Ibid.*, p. 137.
38. *The United Nations* (booklet), Headline Series, No. 59 (New York: Foreign Policy Association, Sept./Oct. 1946), pp. 43–44.
39. John Foster Dulles, *War or Peace* (New York: The Macmillan Company, 1950), p. 40.
40. U Thant, Speech at Upsala, Sweden, May 1962, as quoted in *None Dare Call It Treason* (Florissant: Liberty Bell Press, 1964).
41. *Time* (March 16, 1942), as quoted in *None Dare Call It Treason* (Florissant: Liberty Bell Press, 1964).

42. Willard Cantelon, *The Day the Dollar Dies* (Plainfield: Logos International, 1973), p. 97.
43. Willard Cantelon, *Ibid.*, p. 88.
44. Nate Krupp, *The Omega Generation?* (Arkansas: New Leaf Press, 1977), pp. 78–79.
45. Henry Steele Commager, "Misconceptions Governing American Foreign Policy," *Perspectives on American Foreign Policy* (New York: St Martin's Press, 1983).
46. Robertson, *op. cit.*, pp. 152–153.
47. Robertson, *Ibid.*, p. 172.
48. M. Basilea Schlink, *New Age* (Great Britain: Evangelical Sisterhood of Mary, 1988), p. 7.
49. Constance E. Cumbey, *The Hidden Dangers of the Rainbow: The New Age Movement and Our Coming Age of Barbarism* (Shreveport, Louisiana: Huntington House, Inc., 1983), p. 44.
50. Schlink, *op. cit.*, p. 11.
51. Cumbey, *op. cit.*, p. 63.
52. Cumbey, as quoted by Schlink, *op. cit.*, p. 12.
53. Cumbey, as quoted by Schlink, *Ibid.*, p. 12.
54. Kah, *op. cit.*, p. 69.
55. Kah, *Ibid.*, p. 73.
56. Schlink, *op. cit.*, p. 15.
57. Kah, *op. cit.*, p. 77.
58. Schlink, *op. cit.*, p. 17.
59. Kah, *op. cit.*, p. 77.
60. Christian Warmer, "World Dictatorship and the New Age Movement," *Newswatch Magazine* (Sept. 1986), p. 26.
61. Kah, *op. cit.*, p. 94.
62. Flavius Josephus, *Antiquities of the Jews*, trans. William Whiston, *The Complete Works of Josephus*, Book 1 (Grand Rapids: Kregel Publications, 1960,1978,1981), p. 30.
63. Alexander Hislop, *The Two Babylons of the Papal Worship* (New Jersey: Loizeaux Brothers, 1916), pp. 42–43.
64. Ralph Woodrow, *Babylon Mystery Religion* (California: Ralph Woodrow Evangelistic Association, Inc., 1966), p. 10.
65. Woodrow, *Ibid.*, pp. 10–11.
66. Kah, *op. cit.*, pp. 98–100.
67. Kah, TWA, p. 101.
68. Michael Baigent and Richard Leigh, *The Temple and the Lodge* (London: Corgi Books, 1990), pp. 132–133.
69. Albert G. Mackey, *An Encyclopaedia of Freemasonry* (New York: The Masonic History Co, 1921), p. 842.
70. *The Arizona Daily Star* (February 28,1982), p. 6–A.
71. Epperson, *op. cit.*, p. 79.
72. Nesta Webster, *Secret Societies and Subversive Movements* (New York: EP Dutton, 1924), p. 214.
73. John Robison, *Proofs of a Conspiracy* (Belmont: Western Islands Publishers, 1967), p. 123.
74. Epperson, *op. cit.*, pp. 82–83,
75. Alice Bailey, *The Externalisation of the Hierarchy* (New York: Lucis Publishing Company, 1957), p. 511.
76. Kah, *op. cit.*, p. 89.
77. Caro Cardinal y Rodrigues, *The Mystery of Freemasonry Unveiled* (Hawthorne, CA: Christian Book Club of America, 1971), p. 226.
78. Kah, *op. cit.*, p. 95.

79. Joseph J. Carr, *The Twisted Cross* (Shreveport, Louisiana: Huntington House, Inc., 1985), pp. 110–111.
80. Carr, *Ibid*, p. 93.
81. Carr, *Ibid.*, p. 104.
82. Carr, *Ibid.*, p. 106.
83. Wulf Schwarzwaller, *The Unknown Hitler* (New York: Berkley Books, 1990), p. 99.
84. Schwarzwailer, *Ibid.*, pp. 53–54.
85. Schwarzwailer, *Ibid.*, pp. 56–60.
86. Leo A. Rudloff, *Archbishop Capucci and Terrorism* (booklet) (New York: Anti-Defamation League of B'nai B'rith, 1981).
87. Bernard Lewis, *Semites and Anti-Semites* (London: Weidenfeld and Nicolson, 1986), p. 81.
88. Rudloff, *op. cit.*, p. 10.
89. Neil C. Livingstone and David Halevy, *Inside the PLO* (New York: William Morrow and Co, Inc., 1990), p. 186.
90. Jillian Becker, *The Rise and Fall of the PLO* (London: Weidenfeld and Nicolson, 1987), p. 154.
91. Eliyahu Tal, *PLO: Now the Story Can Be Told* (Tel Aviv: Achduth Press, 1982), pp. 40–41.
92. Becker, *op. cit.*, p. 123.
93. Becker, *Ibid.*, p. 124.
94. *At Magazine* (Aug. 1982), as quoted by Tal, *op. cit.*, p. 43.
95. Tal, *op. cit.*, p. 43.
96. Tal, *Ibid*, p. 45.
97. John Laffin, *The PLO Connections* (London: Corgi Books, 1982), p. 104.
98. Mark Aarons and John Loftus, *Ratlines: How the Vatican's Nazi Networks Betrayed Western Intelligence to the Soviets* (London: Mandarin Paperbacks, 1991), p. 71.
99. Aarons and Loftus *Ibid.*, p. 71.
100. Gowen, Caniglia and Morena, Report of 12 September 1947, USNA, Investigative Records Repository RG319, Pavelic Dossier, XE 001109.
101. Aarons and Loftus, *op. cit.*, p. 76.
102. Aarons and Loftus, *Ibid.*, p. 77.
103. Paul Manning, *Martin Bormann* (New York: Lyle Stuart, 1981), pp. 205–206.
104. David S. Wyman, *The Abandonment of the Jews: America and the Holocaust 1941–1945* (New York: Pantheon Books, 1984), Preface, p. xiii.
105. Wyman, *Ibid*, pp. 317–318.
106. Amir Taheri, *Holy Terror: The Inside Story of Islamic Terrorism* (London: Sphere Books, 1987), p. 196.
107. Richard Nixon, *Seize the Moment* (New York: Simon & Schuster, 1992), p. 198.
108. Taheri, *op. cit.*, p. 198.
109. Taheri, *Ibid.*, p. 199.
110. Muhammad Taqi Partovi Sabzevari, *Ayandeh Nehzat Islami (The Future of the Islamic Movement)*, (Qom 1986).
111. Michael de Semlyen, *Ecumenism: Where Is It Leading Us?* (booklet) (UK: Spirit of '88), p. 3.
112. de Semlyen, *Ibid.*, p. 6.
113. de Semlyen, *Ibid.*, p. 5.
114. Malachi Martin, *The Keys of This Blood: Pope John Paul II Versus Russia and the West for Control of the New World Order* (New York: Touchstone, 1990), Cover.
115. de Semlyen, *op. cit.*, pp. 13–14,19.
116. Martin, *op. cit.*, p. 33.
117. Martin, *Ibid.*, pp. 20–21.

118. Martin, *Ibid.*, p. 33.
119. Martin, *Ibid.*, p. 38.
120. Martin, *Ibid.*, p. 303.
121. Martin, *Ibid.*, p. 299.
122. Martin, *Ibid.*, p. 53.
123. de Semlyen, *op. cit.*, p. 63.
124. William L. Hull, *The Fall and Rise of Israel* (Grand Rapids: Zondervan Publishing House, 1954), pp. 32–33.
125. Rabbi Leibel Reznick, *Woe, Jerusalem* (Kfar Chassidim: Tuvia's Sefarim, 1990), pp. 64–65.
126. Simon Weisenthal, *Every Day Remembrance Day,* pp. 135–137.
127. Michael L. Brown, *Our Hands Are Stained With Blood: The Tragic Story of the "Church" and the Jewish People* (Shippensburg: Destiny Image Publishers, 1992), pp. 104–106.
128. Elie Wiesel, *Night* (New York: Bantam Books, 1982), pp. 60–62.
129. Livia E. Bitton Jackson, *EM: Coming of Age in the Holocaust* (London: Grafton Books, 1984)
130. Jackson, *Ibid,* pp. 176–178.
131. Jean-Francois Steiner, *Treblinka* (New York: Simon & Schuster, 1967), pp. 81–83.
132. Dennis Prager and Joseph Telushkin, *Why the Jews? The Reason for Antisemitism* (New York: Touchstone, 1985), p. 104.
133. Malcolm Hay, *The Roots of Christian Anti-Semitism* (New York: Liberty Press, 1981), p. 21, as quoted in Brown, *op. cit.*, p. 11.
134. Brown, *op. cit.*, p. 11.
135. Leonard Stein, *The Balfour Declaration* (Jerusalem: The Magnes Press, 1983), p. 10.
136. Claude Duvernoy, *The Prince and the Prophet,* Trans. Jack Joffe (Jerusalem: Christian Action For Israel), p. 10.
137. Duvernoy, *Ibid.*, p. 11.
138. Duvernoy, *Ibid.*, p. 9.
139. Duvernoy, *Ibid.*, p. 8.
140. Duvernoy, *Ibid.*, p. 9.
141. Paul Grattan Guinness, *Hear O Israel* (New York: Vantage Press, 1983), p. 17.
142. Guinness, *Ibid.*, p. 89.
143. ICEJ, Christian Zionist Congress, Jerusalem, April 1988.
144. Theodor Herzl, as quoted in Lance Lambert, *The Uniqueness of Israel* (Eastbourne: Kingsway Publications, 1980), p. 128.
145. Lambert, *Ibid.*, p. 132.
146. Theodor Herzl, *The Jewish State* (Bedford: Swann and Ibbitt, 1936), p. 79.
147. Guinness, *op. cit.*, p. 83.
148. Lord Russell, *If I Forget Thee* (London: Cassell & Co., 1960), p. 23.
149. Guinness, *op. cit.*, p. 82.
150. Josef Fraenkel, *Theodor Herzl* (London: Ararat Publishing Society, 1946), p. 145.
151. Yom-Tov L. Hel-Or, *Israel's Spiritual Ethical Renaissance* (Jerusalem: Or Yerushalayim, 1977), p. 22.
152. Claude Duvernoy, *The Zionism of God* (Jerusalem: Ahva Press, 1985), p. 114.
153. Peggy Mann, Golda: *The Life of Israel's Prime Minister* (New York: Coward, McCann & Geoghegan, 1971), pp. 69–70.
154. Menachem Begin, *White Nights: The Story of a Prisoner in Russia* (Tel Aviv: Steimatzkys, 1977), pp. 197–198,200–201.
155. Barnet Litvinoff, *Weizmann: Last of the Patriarchs* (London: Hodder & Stoughton, 1976), p. 26.

156. Robert St. John, *Tongue of the Prophets* (New York: Country Life Press, 1952), p. 354.
157. Claude Duvernoy, *op. cit.,* p. 155.
158. Joan Peters, *From Time Immemorial: The Origins of the Arab-Jewish Conflict Over Palestine* (London: Michael Joseph, 1984), p. 132.
159. *The Covenant of the Islamic Resistance Movement* (August 1988).
160. Peters, *op. cit.,* p. 240.
161. James Gardner, *The Faiths of the World: An Account of All Religions and Religious Sects* (London: A. Fullarton & Co.), Vol. 1, p. 462.
162. Bat Ye'or, *The Dhimmi: Jews and Christians Under Islam* (Cranbury: Associated University Presses, 1985).
163. BatYe'or, *Les Chretiente D'Orient Entre Jihad Et Dhimmitude* (Paris: Les Editions du Cerf, 1991).
164. Bat Ye'or, *op. cit.,* pp. 45–46.
165. Bat Ye'or, *op. cit.,* p. 139.
166. Peters, *op. cit.,* p. 34.
167. Radio Damascus, 15 March 1971.
168. Becker, *op. cit.,* p. 173.
169. *Al Riyadh* (29 January 1981), in J.P.S. 39:184.
170. Anis A. Shorrosh, *Islam Revealed: A Christian Arab's View of Islam* (Nashville: Thomas Nelson Publishers, 1988), p. 185.
171. Peters, *op. cit.,* p. 172.
172. Peters, *Ibid.,* p. 173.
173. David Pryce-Jones, *The Closed Circle: An Interpretation of the Arabs* (London: Paladin, 1990), pp. 205–206.
174. Terence Prittie and Bernard Dineen, *The Double Exodus* pp. 6–8.
175. Yitschak Ben Gad, *Politics, Lies and Videotape* (New York: Shapolsky, 1991), pp. 316–317.
176. A. Y. Levanon, "Three Memorial Prayers in Jerusalem," *Written in Battle: The Six Day War as Told by the Fighters Themselves* (Tel Aviv: Le-Dory Publishing House), pp. 72, 81–83.
177. Guela Cohen, *Voice of Valor* (Tel Aviv: Yair Publishers, 1990), pp. 268–269.
178. Eliyahu Tal, "Whose Jerusalem?" a draft, (The International Forum for a United Jerusalem), p. 45.

The Jerusalem Newswire

Whether you are a Christian or Jewish leader, academic, politician, professional, homemaker, businessman or student, the ebb and flow of events in the Middle East affects your life. Two thousand years ago, Israel was at the center of the world stage. Today, against all human odds and despite the many conflicts tearing at other nations around the globe, the tiny Jewish state once again holds that pivotal position.

The Arab-Israeli conflict has received more media coverage than any other struggle in the world, and it is therefore expected that most people would be aware of the true nature of the strife. But the historical facts behind this conflict are consistently warped and twisted—even in authoritative reference works—and contemporary news coverage of the situation is largely uneven, displaying a marked bias against Israel in favor of the Arab parties involved.

Amid the media torrent flooding the world from Jerusalem, a news service exists that strives to put political events in the Middle East in an accurate biblical and contemporary perspective. The *Jerusalem Newswire* taps Israeli and other media sources, viewing the material through a biblical lens, and presenting its news from that age old perspective. The *Jerusalem Newswire* is not affected or intimidated by Arab or western diplomatic pressure, sanction or censorship. It does not parrot Israeli government policy either, respecting the democratic process whereby Israelis choose their leaders, but duty-bound to speak the truth at all times, even when it goes against the flow of majority Israeli opinion. All its reports and comments are written from that standpoint.

If you are interested in what is happening in Israel, fed up with erroneous and misleading reports, and open to reading a biblical perspective on the events occurring in the most volatile region in the world, email or write to:

The Editor / Jerusalem Newswire
P.O. Box 8817
91860 Jerusalem Israel
Email: editor@jnewswire.com
Website: www.jnewswire.com

Visit the ICZC (**International Christian Zionist Center**) website for relevant articles and helpful, up-to-date insights and information:
Website: www.israelmybeloved.com